Rise of the Maratha Power

D1880089

Owing to the antiquity and rarity of this book, certain pages are regrettably absent, and readability is compromised due to the blurring of the original text. If you possess any insights regarding the availability of these missing sections, kindly inform us. Your assistance is crucial in ensuring the completion of this significant work for the benefit of future generations.

Rise of the Maratha Power.

BY

M. G. RANADE, M.A., LL.B., C.I.E. &c.

GYAN

Published by

Gyan Publishing House
5, Ansari Road
Daryaganj, New Delhi-110002
Phone: 011-47034999, 9811692060
E-mail: books@gyanbooks.com

Distribution Network
gyanbooks.com
India, USA, Canada, UK, Australia

© Publisher

All rights reserved. No part of this work may be reproduced, stored, adapted, or transmitted in any form or by any means, electronic, mechanical, photocopying, micro-filming, recording or otherwise, or translated in any language, without the prior written permission of the copyright owner and the publisher.

ISBN: 978-93-6208-186-5 (PB)
First Published, 1900

2nd Impression 2024

Printed at: Gyan Press, Delhi.

The book is sold subject to the condition that it shall not, by way of trade or otherwise, be lent, resold, hired out, or otherwise circulated without the prior publisher's written consent.

RISE OF THE MARATHA POWER
Author: M. G. RANADE

Rise of the Maratha Power.

BY

M. G. RANADE, M.A., LL.B., C.I.E. &c.,

Judge of her Majesty's High Court of Judicature, Bombay.

Publishers:

PUNALEKAR & Co.,

GIRGAUM, BOMBAY.

1900.

(All Rights Reserved.)

THE Publishers think it their duty to acknowledge their gratitude to the Honble. Mr. Justice M. G. RANADE, for his permitting them to publish the first edition of this volume.

They are also indebted to Mr. N. M. Samarth, B.A., LL.B., High Court Pleader, who kindly undertook the revision of the proof-sheets as they were passing through the Press.

CONTENTS.

PREFACE BY THE AUTHOR.

IT was in the first quarter of the seventeenth century that two apparently insignificant events occurred on the Western Coast of India—the establishment of an English Factory at Surat in 1612, and the birth in 1627 at Shivnér, near Junnar, of a son to a petty Maráthá Jahágirdár of the Ahmednagar Nizám Sháhi Kingdom. Though neither of these events attracted much notice at the time, they heralded the birth of two mighty powers, which were brought into strange contact with one another during the next two centuries, and now as allies, and again as foes, they competed for supremacy in India, till at last the more organized foreign power prevailed in the struggle, and displaced the disorganized native power from its position as supreme ruler. The object of the following narrative is to present to the English and Indian reader a bird's eye view of the history of the rise and progress of the latter power—the power of the Maráthá Confederacy, which, for one hundred years at least, occupied the foremost place among the native rulers of the country, and whose orders were obeyed at one and the same time far off in the west at Dwárká, in the east at Jagannáth, at Haridwár in the north, and Rámêshwar in the south of the Indian Continent. It is not intended to go over the beaten tracks of the detailed story, which has been so elaborately treated in our native Bakhars, and authoritatively described by Mr. Grant Duff, the historian of the Maráthás. Materials for a fuller account of the detailed narrative are being made available by the labours of our native scholars, and they will have in time to be worked up systematically, but the limits assigned to these stray chapters on Maráthá History would of themselves preclude any such ambition. My aim is rather to present a clear view of the salient features of the history from the Indian standpoint, to remove many misapprehensions which detract much from the moral interest and the political lessons of the story, and, above all, to enlist the sympathy of the representatives of the conquering British power in the fortunes of its worsted rival. Now that all jealousies are laid at rest, the tribute of justice may well be paid to the departed great, whose names are cherished by millions in India as the sweet memories of an irrevocable past.

The writer of these chapters claims no other merit for his work. He would not have undertaken the responsibility connected with it but for the fact that it has been handed over to him as a legacy by a revered friend, since deceased, who had, jointly with him, undertaken the work from a feeling of true patriotism, and who would, if he had been spared, have worthily completed, what he no doubt intended to be, the *magnum opus* of his brilliant career.

The twelve chapters which are now published relate to the rise of the Maráthá Power. The second volume will treat about the progress of the confederacy. The manuscript notes are nearly ready; but as, since these notes were first written, the Government of Bombay has made available to the public the records in the Poona Daftar, it has been deemed advisable to delay the publication of these succeeding chapters for the present. When such fresh materials have been made available, it would not be proper to write on this part of the subject without a careful study of these hitherto-neglected sources of information. At the desire of appreciative friends, a contribution from the pen of the late Mr. Justice Telang is added at the end as a fitting conclusion to this volume. Mr. Telang's paper, "Gleanings from the Maráthá Chronicles," represents the true spirit in which native historians should treat the past history of their country. As this work presupposes a general acquaintance with the facts of Maráthá History, and only seeks to suggest and enforce its lessons, it has not been deemed necessary to overload the book by references to English and Native authorities. The lessons it seeks to illustrate are (1) that the rise of the Maráthá power was not a mere accident due to any chance combination, but was a genuine effort on the part of a Hindu nationality, not merely to assert its independence, but to achieve what had not been attempted before—the formation of a Confederacy of States animated by a common patriotism, and (2) that the success it achieved was due to a general upheaval social, religious, and political of all classes of the population. The attempt failed; but even the failure was itself an education in the highest virtues, and possibly intended to be a preparatory discipline to cement the union of the Indian races under British guidance.

CHAPTER I.

The Importance of Maráthá History.

IT may be well to state at the outset in a concise form what is the moral import of the story we have to narrate, and why such a prominent place is claimed for the History of the Maráthá Confederacy above all other similar narratives of many Native Dynasties and Powers with a longer pedigree and a more chequered career. There are many who think that there can be no particular moral significance in the story of the rise and fall of a freebooting Power, which thrived by plunder and adventure, and succeded only because it was the most cunning and adventurous among all those who helped to dismember the Great Moghul Empire after the death of Aurangzéb. This is a very common feeling with the readers, who derive their knowledge of these events solely from the works of English historians. Even Mr. Grant Duff has given his support to the view that "the turbulent predatory spirit of the Hindus of Maháráshtra, though smothered for a time, had its latent embers stirred by the contentions of their Mahomedan Conquerors, till, like the parched grass kindled amid the forests of the Sahyádri mountains, they burst forth in spreading flame, and men afar off wondered at the conflagration." If this view of the historian be correct, it may fairly be urged that there is nothing in the narrative which can be described as having a moral significance useful for all time. The sequel of this narrative will, however, it is hoped, furnish grounds which will lead the historical student of Modern India to the conclusion that such a view is inconsistent with facts, and that the mistake is of a sort which renders the whole story unintelligible. Any one who sees no distinction between the great leaders who helped in the work of building up the Maráthá Confederacy and the careers of Hyder and Tipu in Mysore, of Nizám-ul-Mulk at Hyderábád, Sujá-ud-oulá in Oudh, Alivardikhán in Bengal, Ranjitsingh in the Punjáb and Surajmall in Bhartpur, will never be able to occupy the correct stand-point of vision from which this history must be studied, and he will fail to understand its real import as signally as any native student, who tried to account for the British ascendency in India by crediting the whole success to the adventurous spirit of Clive or the diplomacy of Hastings, forgetting all the while that this adventure and diplomacy only achieved success because they were backed up by the resolution and persistence and resources of the great British Nation. Freebooters and adventurers never succeed in building up empires, which last for generations and permanently alter the political map of a great Continent. Unlike the great *Subhédárs* of Provinces, who became independent after the death of Aurangzéb, the Founder of the Maráthá Power and his successors for two generations bore the brunt of the attack of the Moghul Empire at the zenith of its splendour. The military adventurers named above were not backed up by any national force behind them, and their power perished with the individuals who founded it. In the case of the Maráthá Confederacy, however, it was far otherwise. For ten generations a succession of great leaders sprang up to fill up the place of those who died in the struggle, and the Confederacy not only outlived opposition but derived greater strength from the reverses it sustained from time to time, rising Phœnix-like in greater splendour from the very ashes of its apparent ruin. This tenacity shewed clearly that the underlying principles had stronger vitality than can be explained by the standard theory of adventure and freebooting, or the illustration of a sudden conflagration. We shall attempt in this chapter to state briefly these distinguishing features, which lend to the story all the moral and permanent interest it possesses for the student of History.

I. In the first place it should be noted that the immediate predecessors of the British Rulers of India were not the Mahomedans, as is too often taken for granted, but they were the Native Rulers of the country, who had successfully thrown off the Mahomedan yoke. Mr. Grant Duff, indeed, claims for Maráthá History this particular feature of interest, and describes the Maráthás as "our predecessors in conquest in India, whose power was gradually gaining strength, before it found a head in the far-famed adventurer, Shivájí Bhonslé." Except in Bengal and on the Coromándel Coast, the Powers displaced by the English conquest were not Mahomedan *Subhédárs*, but native Hindu Rulers who had successfully asserted their independence.

Among these Native Powers, the first place must be assigned to the members of the Maráthá Confederacy. The Maráthá Power took its rise in Western Mahárástra, and the sphere of its influence soon extended to the Central Deccan, Karnátik, and Southern India as far south as Tanjore, including Mysore. On the north it embraced Gujarát including Káthiáwád, Bérárs, Central Provinces up to Katak, Málwá in Central India, Bundélkhand, Rajputáná, Northern Indian including Delhi, Agrá, the Doáb and Rohilkhand. Bengal and Oudh were invaded, but were protected from conquest solely by the interposition of the British armies. For fifty years the Emperors at Delhi were made or unmade by the agents of this Power. In the whole of the territory included within these limits, the power was in the hands of Native Chiefs, who were either members of the Confederacy or old rulers in subordinate alliances with the Confederacy. The two buffer Mahomedan States at Hyderábád and Mysore were completely under the same influence. The secret of a combination which extended its sway over such a vast territory, and held it together for over a century, cannot but be a matter of absorbing interest to the British Rulers of India. The recognized head of the Confederacy was the *Péshwá*, who was not only the chief military leader in his own country, but was also the deputy to the Delhi Emperors kept prisoners in the Moghul Palace. For all practical purposes, therefore, it may be safely stated that, except in Bengal and on the Madrás Coast, the chief power in the country was in the hands of the Native Hindu Rulers controlled by the Confederacy. The Mahomedan influence had spent itself, and the Hindus had asserted their position and become Independent Rulers of the country, with whom alone the British Power had to contend for supremacy.

II. The secret of this combination cannot be properly understood without a full recognition of the fact that it was not the work of one man, or of a succession of gifted men. The foundation was laid broad and deep in the hearts of the whole people. Unlike the *Subhédárships* of Bengal, Karnátik, Oudh, and Hyderábád, the rise of the Maráthá Power was due to the first beginnings of what one may well call the process of nation-making. It was not the outcome of the successful enterprise of any individual adventurer. It was the upheaval of the whole population, strongly bound together by the common affinities of language, race, religion and literature, and seeking further solidarity by a common independent political existence. This was the first experiment of the kind attempted in India after the disastrous period of foreign Musalman invasions. As a first effort, it was wanting in that solidity of structure which has characterised the great European nations, but there can be no mistake about this being its essential and distinguishing feature. It was a national movement or upheaval in which all classes co-operated. The strength of the organization did not depend on a temporary elevation of the higher classes, but it had deeper hold on the vast mass of the rural population. Cowherds and shepherds, Bráhmans and non-Bráhmans, even Musalmans felt its influence and acknowledged its power. European writers, who have condemned the Indian races for their want of a national feeling, have themselves been forced to admit exceptions in the case of the Maráthás, Rajputs, and Sikhs. With the Rajputs, the ascendency was confined to a few particular clans of noble families. With the Sikhs, the ascendency was limited to the *Khálsá* army, who constituted a small minority of the population of the Punjáb. The case was far otherwise with the Maráthás, among whom there were, no doubt, class ascendencies and clannish feelings, but these were kept under by the political sense of the population generally, who joined the national armies for six months in the year, and returned to their homes, and cultivated their family lands, and enjoyed their *Vatans* during the remaining period. This regard for the *Vatans* in the old country has been a marked feature of Maráthá character, and even the Commanders of great armies prided themselves more upon their being *Pátils* and *Déshmukhs* in their old villages in Maháráshtra than on their extensive *Jahágirs* in distant lands. This feeling of patriotism illustrates most forcibly the characteristic result of the formation of a Nation in the best sense of the word, and constitutes another reason why the History of the Maráthás deserves special study. It is the history of the formation of a true Indian Nationality, raising its head high above the troubled waters of Mahomedan confusion. It was this force behind, which supported the efforts of the leaders, and enabled them to dream as a possibility the establishment of a central Hindu *Pádsháhi* or Empire at Delhi, uniting and controlling all other Native Powers. The histories of Hyder and Tipu, and of the Mahomedan Rulers of Hyderábád, Karnátik, Bengal and Oudh, present nothing parallel to it. They are personal histories, while the history of the Power associated with the name of Shiváji is very properly called the History of the Maráthás.

III. One more feature of the history has entirely escaped the observation of European writers, though it constitutes perhaps the strongest ground why the study possesses peculiar moral interest to the historical student. It was not a mere Political Revolution that stirred Maháráshtra towards the close of the sixteenth and the commencement of the seventeenth century. The Political Revolution was preceded, and in fact to some extent caused, by a Religious and Social upheaval which moved the entire population. The popular idea that it was Religious Persecution which agitated Mahárúshtra and strengthened the hands of Shiváji and his comrades, is not wholly wrong, but it represents only a partial truth. The Mahomedan Rulers of the Deccan in the fifteenth and sixteenth centuries were not bigoted fanatics. Aurangzèb was, no doubt, a fanatic, but his fanaticism could not explain the rise of a Power which struggled with him on equal terms and secured victory in the end. The fact was that, like the Protestant Reformation in Europe in the sixteenth century, there was a Religious, Social, and Literary Revival and Reformation in India, but notably in the Deccan in the fifteenth and sixteenth centuries. This Religious Revival was not Bráhmanical in its orthodoxy; it was heterodox in its spirit of protest against forms and ceremonies and class distinctions based on birth, and ethical in its preference of a pure heart, and of the law of love, to all other acquired merits and good works. This Religious Revival was the work also of the people, of the masses, and not of the classes. At its head were Saints and Prophets, Poets and Philosophers, who sprang chiefly from the lower orders of society—tailors, carpenters, potters, gardeners, shop-keepers, barbers, and even *mahárs*—more often than Bráhmans. The names of Tukárám, of Rámdás, of Váman Pandit and Eknáth were names to conjure with, and after a lapse of two hundred years, they still retain their ascendency over the minds of the people of Maháráshtra. The Political Leaders acted in concert with these Religious Leaders of the people. Shiváji's chief adviser was Rámdás, who gave the colour to the national flag and introduced a new form of salutation, which displayed at once the religious character of the movement and the independence of the spirit which prompted it. The first Bájiráo Péshwá derived his inspiration from the *Swámi* of Dhúvadshi. Vithal Shivdév, the founder of the Vinchurkar family, was similarly inspired by his Preceptor. Shiváji's character and his motive-springs of action have been more correctly delineated by Colonel Medows Taylor in his novel than by the historian of the Maráthás. Shiváji felt that he had a direct inspiration from the goddess Bhawáni, and in the great crises of his life, he always guided himself by what this inspiration suggested to him in moments of intense possession. These influences deserve special study, because they have left their mark up to the present day on the aspirations and faith of the people. What Protestantism did for Western Europe in the matter of civil liberty was accomplished on a smaller scale in Western India. The impulse was felt in art, in religion, in the growth of vernacular literature, in communal freedom of life, in increase of self-reliance and toleration; and the interest of the study is on this account greatly heightened both to the native student and the foreign inquirer.

IV. One other feature may be noticed, which was at once the strength and the weakness of the Maráthá Power. The history of the Maráthás is a history of confederated States. The central power was always weak after the death of its great founder. Even Shiváji was influenced in his arrangements by his national tendency. He had a Council of Eight Ministers who were more than councillors, being themselves both civil and military leaders. Even in his lifetime, when he was a captive at Delhi, and his country and its forts were in Mahomedan hands, this distribution of power enabled him to raise his head soon after escaping from captivity. When his son, later on, was captured by Aurangzéb's General, the confederate leaders retired to the south, and, again on a suitable occasion, returned and wreaked their vengeance on Aurangzéb. Under the *Péshwás*, this system was developed still further by the establishment of the great Camps of Maráthá Captains at Indore, Gwálior, Dhár, Déwás, Barodá, and Nágpur; and the Bundélkhand Chiefs in Central India, the Patwardhan Chiefs in the South, the Sátárá *Jahágirdárs,* the Bhávés, the Rástés, the Dhulaps, the Angrés, Mánkars, Mahádiks, the Ghorpadés and many others who might be enumerated, had their smaller camps all along the eastern and southern boundaries of the Empire. These were so many centres of power and vitality, and as long as they were animated by a common purpose and a central idea--and they continued to be so animated for nearly a century—their power was irresistible and even the disciplined British army had to dismember the Confederacy before success could be achieved. For a hundred years there was not an expedition to the south or to the north, to the east or to the west, against the Rajputs or the Delhi Emperors, in Rohilkhand, or Oudh or Bengal, against Hyder, or Tipu, or the Nizám, against the Portuguese, or the English, in which the confederate Chiefs did not act together. The ascendency of the *Péshwás* was like the ascendency of the Prussian Monarchy in the German Empire. The Central Authority represented more the idea than the force of the Confederacy. While the old traditions lasted, it enabled the ministers at Ráigad, Sátárá, Vishálgad, Gingi, or Pooná to carry on the government and direct the national force without the advantage always of having any strong personal ruler at the head. The *Péshwá's* Government under Náná Fadnavis was actually nicknamed in the courts at Hyderábád and Shrirangapatan as the *Bár-bhai Government,* or the Government of the Confederacy of Twelve Leaders. When the idea ceased to be respected, the Confederacy proved a source of weakness rather than strength. The English rulers knew this weakness, and took advantage of it by appealing to the selfish vanity of each member of the Confederacy separately, and thus loosened its joint force. There was no such experiment of Federal Government on such a large scale undertaken in this country under either Hindu or Mahomedan sovereigns. The experiment was doomed to ultimate failure, for it presupposed virtues which are not hereditary, but as long as these virtues had the ascendency, it had redeeming features of its own which enhance the value of the study to the native and foreign historian.

V. The moral interest of the story is further heightened by the fact that the Confederacy arrangements enabled the Maráthá nation to outlive and grow stronger from the very reverses it sustained during the critical periods of its history. There were four such critical periods :—

i. when Shiváji became a prisoner at Delhi ;

ii. when Sambháji was taken captive, and his brother Rájárám had to retreat to the south ;

iii. when the battle of Pánipat apparently destroyed all hopes of Maráthá ascendency ;

iv. when Náráyanráo Péshwá was murdered, and the Ministers had to set aside Rághobá and carry on the administration with a house divided against itself, and with the whole force of the British Power to oppose.

A nation that could stand four such reverses and catastrophes, and rise superior to them, possesses an interest for the historical student which cannot be adequately measured by the length of time that the Empire lasted.

VI. Lastly, even at the present day, though the British Rulers of India occupy the place of the *Péshwás* and of the Moghul Emperors as suzerain power, to which all other States are subject, the remnants of the Confederacy that are still in the enjoyment of subordinate independence at Gwálior, Indore, Barodá, Kolhápur, Dhár and Déwás, the Southern Maráthá

Chiefs, and the Maráthá population of about thirty millions included in the Bombay Presidency and the Native States, as also in the Central Provinces, Bérárs, and the Nizám's country, represent a power which is second to none among the native communities and States, which enjoy the protection of, and own allegiance to, the British Rule. This element of present influence cannot also fail to have a deep interest to those who can see far into the future of the possibilities open to a Federated India, distributed according to nationalities, and subjected to a common bond of connection with the Imperial Power of the Queen-Empress of India.

These are the principal features in which centres the permanent moral interest of the story of the rise and fall of the Maráthá Confederacy, which we propose to narrate in the sequel.

CHAPTER II

HOW THE GROUND WAS PREPARED.

ONE of the most ordinary misconceptions on the part both of Native and European writers on Maráthá History is to attribute the rise of the Maráthá Power solely to fortuitous circumstances. Mr. Grant Duff himself in his narrative has compared the rise of the Maráthá Power to a sudden conflagration like those which occur in the forests in Sahyádri. This is, however, not his matured opinion, for he has devoted the first three chapters of his history to trace the foundation of the Power in events which long preceded the birth of the great Shiváji in the early part of the seventeenth century. The fact appears to be that fortuitous circumstances had very little part to play in the early foundation of the Maráthá Power. If we would understand the matter correctly, we must trace these causes to a period long anterior to that of the

2

Mahomedan conquest of the Deccan. The ancient history of Maháráshtra, as gathered from inscriptions on copper-plates and rock-temples, has been laboriously compiled by Indian antiquarians, and these materials have been made available to ordinary readers by Dr. Bhándárkar's compilations on the subject. The questions we have to consider are, (1) why the first successful attempt to throw off the Mahomedan yoke on a large scale was made in Western India, and (2) what were the circumstances in the nature of the country, in the habits and the institutions of the people inhabiting it, which favoured such an attempt, and rewarded it with success.

In this connection, the first point we have to notice is the fact that the country of Mahárashtra enjoys natural advantages of position and climate which are denied to the people of the lowlands and the valleys of the Ganges, the Indus and the other great rivers which flow into the Arabian Sea or the Indian Ocean. The characteristic features of the Mahárashtra country are the great mountain ranges which enclose it on two sides—the Sahyádri range running from north to south, and the Sátpurá and the Vindhyá ranges running from east to west.

The minor ranges, which break out in rugged outline from these mountain chains and form the watersheds of many rivers which fall ultimately into the Godávari and into the Krishná, give the whole country an appearance of ruggedness and unevenness not to be met with in other parts of India on such a scale. Geographically, Maháráshtra includes the Konkan—the strip between the Sahyádri and the sea, the *Ghátmáthá* being the country on the top of the ranges, and the *Désh*, which includes the valleys lower down the river. The hill-forts on the top of these ranges typify and protect the naturally defensible position of the country and they have played an important part in its political history. These characteristic features of the country secure for it the advantages of a good and bracing climate, which distinguishes it from the dry and moist extremes of heat and cold of the temperature of the plains in North India and the lowlands. At the same time, owing to its hilly character, the soil is poor, and the country is sparsely inhabited by a hardy and abstemious people. It is the old story of the Highlands and the Lowlands, the gifts of nature being evenly distributed to all alike on the principle of compensation. The country thus defined forms a sort of a triangle of which the Sahyádri range and the sea, from Daman to Kárwár, form the base; the Sátpurá range forms the perpendicular side, reaching to the east beyond Nagpur as far as the watershed of the Godávari and its tributaries extend, and the hypotenuse which joins these two ranges has been determined not so much by natural features as by the test of language. The area thus marked out exceeds one lac of square miles, and its population comes to about thirty million. The natural features mentioned above, and its position on the high road between Northern India and the Southern Peninsula, give it commanding advantages denied to the other tablelands of Mysore and Málwá, which alone can be compared with it.

Next to these natural features, the history of the country has been dominated by the character of the people. In Northern India, the element of the Aryan race has predominated to an extent which dwarfed the aboriginal races, and drove them into the hilly parts of the country. In the Southern Peninsula, the *Dravidian* races have retained their predominant position, the *Aryan* element being not powerful enough to impress its stamp upon the population generally. By reason of its position between the two divisions now mentioned, the table-land of Maháráshtra has been inhabited by a population in which the *Áryans* and the *Dravidians* have been mixed in due proportion, so as to retain the good points of both without exaggerating their defects. This mixture of the two elements is best illustrated by the peculiarities of the language, whose base is *Dravidian*, but whose growth and structure have been entirely fashioned by *Aryan* influences. In their physiognomy the people are not as fair, soft or well proportioned, as the people in Northern India are; neither are they as black and hard-featured as the Southern *Dravidian* races. The *Áryan* element itself includes in Maháráshtra a due mixture of the first settlers, as also of the subsequent Scythian invaders. The non-*Áryans* similarly include the Aboriginals, *Bhils*, *Kolis* and *Rámoshis* and other low classes, as also the higher *Dravidian* elements.

Owing to this due proportion of the different ethnic elements in the population, the institution and the religion of the country have maintained an equilibrium which is rarely found in other parts of India. Among these institutions the system of village communities is most characteristic, and has been developed to a point which has enabled it to survive all foreign interference that has proved so fatal elsewhere. The village community with the *Pancháyat* system has been maintained up to the present day in a manner to subserve the highest aims of government, and has become an integral part of the present system of administration, which has found it so useful as to introduce it in a modified form both in Sind and Gujarát, in which provinces the Mahomedan influence was so predominant as to destroy village autonomy. Along with the village and *Pancháyat* systems, the *Ryot-wári mirási* tenure of land, held in full ownership by small peasant proprietors directly responsible to the State, has given a stability and a sense of independence to the ryots which is rarely met with in other provinces. While the village organization has thus been kept up intact, the system of higher revenue management by means of hereditary *Déshmukhs* and *Déshpándés* has not outlived the purpose for which it was originally instituted. The *Déshmukhs* and the *Désáis* in other parts of the country have developed into Bengal *Zamindárs* and Oudh *Táluk-dárs,* who made themselves directly responsible to the State, and became in the end owners of village lands. The village communities in North and North-Western India similarly are distinguished from the village organization in Maháráshtra by those communities retaining joint responsibility and ownership, which have given place to individual property in Maháráshtra. The tenure of land is thus of a more equal and almost democratic character than in other parts of the country. Owing to these peculiarities, the people have retained habits of mutual helpfulness and independence which have stood them to good account in past times.

Along with these civil institutions, the popular religion of the country has avoided the extremes of sectarianism which disfigure and disunite the *Dravidian* portion of the peninsula, and the minute sub-divisions of caste which obtain in North India. The *Smárts* and the *Vaishnavs,* the orthodox and the heterodox, do not present in Maháráshtra those exaggerated differences which strike one as soon as he crosses the Tunga-bhadra river. If not blended together, they show tolerance of a sort amounting almost to indifference, which is characteristic of the country. The Bráhmans and the non-Bráhman *Shudrás* are brought into contact on more equal terms than elsewhere. There are neither *Goswámis* or *Mahants* or *Gurus* whose influence runs side by side with Bráhmans eleswhere. The fact is that the so-called *Shudrás* have, under the influence of the *Vaishnav* saints, emancipated themselves from the low social position assigned to them in the old writings, and have risen to be either *Kshatriyás* or *Vaishyás*, according as they followed the professions of war or of peace. The *Shudrás* and even the Pariahs—*Mahárs*—have produced saints and poets whose names are revered by the whole country, Bráhmans included. Even the Mahomedans lose their bigoted character under these same moderating influences. The Hindus make common cause with Mahomedans in their great festivals, and this feeling is reciprocated by the Musalmans, except where influences from North India intervene. Some Mahomedan *Fakirs* have been ranked with the Hindu saints in general veneration, and there are some saints who are venerated by both communities alike. These features of tolerance and moderation have been developed in the course of centuries and they constitute some of the most stable elements of the national character.

Owing to the nature of the country, and the character of its people and their institutions as described above, the sense of local autonomy and independence has been developed to an extent which prevented the country from being retained under one political control for a long time, both under Hindu and Mahomedan rulers. We hear of great empires in Northern and Eastern India, as also in the Southern Peninsula, but the essential feature of political arrangements in Maháráshtra has been separatistic, and in conflict with the long continuation of centralized power. This separatist tendency has not prevented the people from joining together to repel attacks from the northern invaders. Ancient traditions credit Sháliwáhan or Shátawáhan with having repelled one such attack of Scythian invaders about the commencement of the Christian era. Another such attack was repelled six hundred years later by another native Maháráshtra ruler, the great Pulkéshi of the first Chálukya dynasty. The country was parcelled out into small principalities and kingdoms, and its early history, so far as it has been preserved in inscriptions and tablets and coins, shows a perpetual flux of power from one centre to another. Tagárá, Paithan, Badámi, Málkhéd, Goá, Kolhápur,

Kalyáni, Dévgiri or Daulatábád and other places were successively seats of the earlier and later Chálukyás and Ráshtrakutás and the Yádav kings; and the Chálukyás, the Nalawadés, the Kadambs, the Morés, Shilhars, the Ahirs, the Yádavs, and other clans fought for supremacy with one another. This state of things continued till the advent of the Mahomedan power, which was established for two hundred years in Northern India before it invaded the Deccan about the commencement of the fourteenth century. It took the Mahomedans nearly thirty years before the Hindu powers in the open plains were subdued. The subjugation was never completed so far as Western Maháráshtra and Konkan are concerned. Konkan was not conquered till the middle of the fifteenth century and the Ghátmáthá, or the Mávals were never conquered in the sense in which the Désh country was brought under Mahomedan yoke.

The Mahomedan influence, as measured by the change in the habits and the language of the people, was scarcely perceptible in these hilly parts of the western country, which were ruled by Hindu commanders of hill-forts. Measured by numbers, the same influence appears to have been least perceptible in these parts, for the Mahomedan population even now shows the smallest percentages in Western Mahárásh-tra. The Mahomedan domination never acquired any strong or permanent hold over the country in these parts. In Northern and Eastern India, white mosques and mausoleums towered high, the Hindu temples were scarcely tolerated in the largest centres of the population, and were huddled into street corners, and the worship had to be performed in stealth and secrecy. In North India the Mahomedan language and letters impressed themselves upon the country till they penetrated into every home and bazaar, and gave rise to the modern Urdu; no such changes took place in Maháráshtra, and the language and religion of the people continued to thrive and develop even under Moslem rule.

It would be interesting in this place to note the successive steps by which the Mahomedan power in the Deccan was gradually subverted by, and subordinated to, Hindu influences.

In the first place, the Deccan Mahomedans, being separated by great distances from their base beyond the North-West frontier, were not recruited by fresh invaders, as was the case at Delhi, where Afgháns, Gilchis, Turks, Usbégs, and Moghuls succeeded one another, keeping up the Mahomedan tradition intact with every fresh invasion. In the Deccan this influence was wanting; and the Turks and the Persians and the Abyssinian adventurers were not regularly recruited from time to time.

Secondly.—The founder of the Bahámani Kingdom was a slave of a Bráhman named Gangu at Delhi, who foretold the good fortune that was in store for him. Hassan, the slave, gratefully recognised his obligation when he rose to power, and he called his empire, the "Bahámani Kingdom," and himself Hassan Gangu Bahámani. This in itself was an homage paid to Hindu influences, which distinguished the Deccan Mahomedans from those of the north, and which practically bore fruit, when Gangu was brought over from Delhi, and placed in charge of the Finance Department.

Thirdly.—In consequence of this arrangement, the Revenue management and the charge of the Treasury remained all along in Hindu hands,—Bráhmans and Khatris from

Delhi, and these, in due course of time, made way for the Deccan Bráhmans and Prabhus.

Fourthly.—Not only was the Revenue management in native hands, but later on, when the Bahámani made away for the five separated kingdoms of Bijápur, Bérárs, Ahmednagar, Bédar, and Golcondá, the revenue accounts of villages and *maháls* were kept in the vernacular in place of the foreign Persian or Urdu language.

Fifthly.—There was another way in which the Hindu influence operated upon the Mahomedan kingdom in the Deccan. The revolt in 1347 against the Delhi Emperor, Mahomed Taghlak, though a conspiracy of Mahomedan nobles, became successful chiefly by reason of the alliance of the Hindu kings of Télangan and Vijaynagar with the rebels. The Hindu kingdom in Télangan was subsequently subverted by the Bahámani kings, but the kingdom of Vijaynagar continued to be a strong power for nearly two centuries, till it was finally conquered by the alliance of the five Mahomedan rulers in the battle of Tálikot in 1564. This Hindu power thus exerted, both in peace and in war, considerable influence on the fortunes of the Mahomedan kings, and at times it proved itself too strong even for the united armies of Golcondá and Ahmednagar. The third Bahámani king was forced to enter into an agreement with the Vijaynagar king, by which the indiscriminate slaughter of unarmed people, after a pitched battle, was prohibited on both sides, and the prohibition was enforced for a hundred years without any violation of the compact.

Sixthly.—In consequence of this balance of power between Hindus and Musalmans, the latter seldom indulged in those excesses which distingushed their rule in Northern India, and the former never suffered the depressions they felt elsewhere as an incidence of foreign conquest. Mahomedan troops entered the Vijaynagar service when dissatisfied with their own masters, and the Maráthá *Siledárs* and *Bárgirs* freely enrolled themselves first as auxiliaries, and latterly as the most powerful contingent in the contending armies. The second Bahámani king had a bodyguard of two hundred *Siledárs*. This training in arms brought education, power, and wealth with it, and in the sixteenth century we meet with Ghádgés and Ghorpadès, Jádhavs and Nimbálkars, Morés and Sindés, Daflés and

Mánés, as Generals in charge of ten or twenty thousand horse, and in the enjoyment of proportionate *Jahágirs*. The foreign mercenaries—Turks, Persians, Abyssinians, and Moghuls—proved more troublesome than useful, and gradually reliance came to be placed chiefly upon the country *Bárgirs* and *Silédár* troops.

Seventhly.—Another influence was also operating in the same direction. The Mahomedan rulers in the Deccan took Hindu wives in their harems. The seventh Bahámani king allied himself with the Vijaynagar family, and the ninth Bahámani king married the daughter of the *Rájá* of Sonkhéd. The first Bijápur king, Yusaf Adilsháh, took for his wife the sister of one Mukundráo, a Bráhman, and this lady became his chief queen, being known by the name of Bubuji Khánum, and her sons ascended the throne after Yusaf's death The first ruler of the Barid dynasty at Bédar got his son married to the daughter of one Sábáji Maráthá, who was a nobleman of some note in the service of the Bahámani kings.

Eighthly.—In the same category must be placed the influence of Hindu converts. The first Ahmednagar king was the son of a converted Bráhman *Kulkarni* of Pátri in Bérár, whose family had entered the service of the Vijaynagar kings. The Bráhman surname Bhairav became Béhri the distinguishing title of these kings, and they so faithfully remembered their origin that they conquered Pátri and gave it in *inám* to the Bráhman *Kulkarnis* after a long struggle with the Bérár rulers. The first founder of the Imádsháhi dynasty in Bérár was also the son of a Bráhman in the service of Vijaynagar, who was taken captive and became a convert. In a similar way the first Bédar king of the Barid dynasty was so loved by his Maráthá soldiery that four hundred Maráthás became Mahomedans, and were his most trusted soldiers.

Ninthly.—These influences exerted a power which made it impossible for the Mahomedan powers to retain their bigotry and fanatic cruelty in the Deccan, and although there were irruptions of violence now and then, on the whole great toleration was shown towards their Hindu subjects by these Mahomedan kings, and gradually both civil and military power came into Hindu hands. As a consequence, the Mahomedan kings gave *inàm* land to Hindu temple endowments, and Hindu physicians were employed in hospitals, and in some cases, even grants were given and continued to Bráhman communities. One Murárráo was chief minister at Golcondá about the middle of the sixteenth century, and one Madan Pandit was similarly a minister in the reign of the last Golcondá ruler, and he effected an alliance between Shiváji and the Golcondá kings against the Moghuls. The *Ráj-rái* family was also of considerable importance in Golcondá. Bráhman *Déshpándés* and Maráthá *Déshmukhs* or *Désáis* were placed in charge of district collections, and the names of Dádopant, Narso Kálé, and Yésu Pandit are distinguished for the great reforms they introduced in Bijápur revenue management. Bráhman ambassadors were employed by Ahmednagar kings as envoys in the Courts of Gujarát and Málwá, and a Bráhman minister of *Péshwá*, named Kamalsén, had chief power at Ahmednagar in the times of the first Buransháh. Yésu Pandit also became *Mustápha* in the Bijápur kingdom about the same time. Two Bráhman brothers, Akanná and Makanná, were similarly raised to power in Golcondá, and their services were deemed to be so valuable that the Bijápur kings sought their help when pressed by the Moghul invaders.

Tenthly.—In the Military Department this predominance of the Hindus more and more manifested itself as years rolled on. The names of Kámrájé, Ghádgé, and Harnáik are noted by *Féristá* as being the first Maráthá *Mansubdárs* employed by the Bahámani kings. The second Bahámani king had a bodyguard of two hundred *Silédárs.* The famous Wághoji Jagdévráo Náik played in the first quarter of the sixteenth century a most prominent part in the Courts of Golcondá, Bérár, and Vijaynagar. He made and unmade kings, was in charge of all the *Náikwádi* Hindu forces in the Karnátik, and was a king all but in name. The famous Murárráo Jagdév served the Bijápur kings with great distinction in the early part of the seventeenth century. He resisted the Moghul invasions, and he and Shaháji Bhonslé were the chief supports of the power of Bijápur and Ahmednagar respectively. In the intrigues which brought about Murárráo's downfall, three other Maráthás—Rághopant, a Bráhman, one Bhonslé *Sardár,* and one Ghádgé—figured prominently. Under Murárráo, Chandraráo Moré and Rájáráo rose to distinction in the wars of the Konkan. The families of the Mánés of Mhaswad, the Sávants of Wádi, and the Daflés, and finally the

Ghorpadés, similarly rose to great power in these times.

Mr. Grant Duff mentions the names of eight Maráthá families who rose to power and influence long before Shiváji was born, or before Shaháji's father Máloji rose to any distinction. The most powerful among the families was that of the Jádhav's of Sindkhéd in the Bérárs, who were supposed to be connected with the Dévgiri Jádhavs whom Alá-ud-din had conquered. Lakhoji Jádhav was a person of such importance that his support was sought by the Moghul Emperors when they first invaded the Deccan. The Nimbálkars of Faltan were similarly distinguished. The Ghádgé Zunjárráo of Málawdi belonged to a family of great note in the Bijápur service. The Morés, the Shirkés, the Mahádiks in the Konkan and Ghátmáthá and the Gujars, and the Mohités in the lower Mávals were great commanders, some of them being in charge of ten to twenty thousand horse. The family of Bhonslés was one of those Maráthá families who came to prominence in the beginning of the seventeenth century, being connected with the Jádhavs and Nimbálkars. Sháhaji's mother was a daughter of the Jádhavs, and Sháháji's wife a daughter of the Nimbálkars. The founder of the family was Máloji Bhonslé and his son Shaháji secured a position of the first rank. Shaháji indeed was a king-maker, and on behalf of the Nizámsháhi kings of Ahmednagar kept up the fight with the Moghuls after the second conquest of Ahmednagar.

In consequence of the influences and changes noted above about the commencement of the seventeenth century, the nominal Mahomedan Rulers of Golcondá, Bijápur, Nagar and Bédar were virtually controlled both in the civil and military departments by Maráthá statesmen and Maráthá warriors, and the hill-forts near the *Gháts* and the country thereabout were in the hands of Maráthá *Jahágirdárs,* who were only nominally dependent upon these Mahomedan sovereigns. It was when this slow process of national emancipation was being peacefully worked out that a new danger threatened the country in the attempts made by the Delhi Emperors, from Akbar to Aurangzéb, to extend the Mahomedan power again to the south of the Narmadá and the Tápti rivers. If successful, it would have thrown back the country for another period of three hundred years, which had been the time that the Hindus had taken to re-assert their independence after the first conquest. This new danger was much more formidable as it was backed up by all the resources of the Delhi Empire. This danger was felt to be formidable alike by the Mahomedan rulers of the Deccan and their Maráthá nobles. The separatist tendencies among the Maráthás disabled them from facing the Moghuls in the open field, and the hide-and-seek guerilla system of warfare adopted by the Maráthá armies as their characteristic tactics was under the circumstances unavoidable. The first shock of the Mahomedan invasion had been borne and surmounted, and the country had during the last three hundred years shown a considerable rallying power. The old system of playing the waiting game and allowing the Mahomedan rulers to dissolve themselves in luxury would not have served the purpose. The new danger required new tactics, but above all tactics, what was wanted was a new spirit, a common feeling of interest, a common patriotism born of a liberal religious fervour. The scattered power of the Maráthá chiefs had to be united in a confederacy, animated by a common purpose, and sanctified by a common devotion to the country. Shiváji's great merit was that he realized this danger, kept the separatist tendency under control, brought the common forces together in the name of a common religion, and he thus represented in himself, not only the power of the age, but the soul-stirring idea, the highest need and the highest purpose, that could animate the Maráthás in a common cause. He did not create the Maráthá power; that power had been already created, though scattered in small centres all over the country. He sought to unite it for a higher purpose by directing it against the common danger. This was his chief merit and his chief service to the country, and in this consists his chief claim upon the grateful remembrance of his people. It was not for nothing that the people looked up to him as their inspired leader. He felt the inspiration himself, and communicated it to those about him, not only in one generation, but for generations more to come after him, till the idea of re-establishing Hindu power throughout the country was realized at once in the great centres or camps which the Maráthás established in all parts of the Indian Continent. Thus was the ground prepared partly by nature, partly by the ancient history of the country, partly by the religious revival, but chiefly by the long discipline in arms which the country had undergone under Mahomedan rule for three hundred years.

CHAPTER III.

HOW THE SEED WAS SOWN.

THE first quarter of the seventeenth century was a period when men's minds were in an eager state of expectation in the Deccan, and the seed was sown for which the ground had been prepared for more than three centuries in the way described in the last chapter. It may be of use to note the chief features of the political situation about the time when Shiváji, the founder of the Maráthá Confederacy, was born at Shivanér. The Ahmednagar kingdom of the Nizámsháhi dynasty had ceased to exist. After a brave defence of the city, in which Chándbibi distinguished herself, the Moghuls had to withdraw their forces in 1596, but internal factions soon re-asserted themselves, and Chándbibi was murdered in 1599, and the fort was taken by the Moghul armies and the king was sent a prisoner to Barhánpur. The adherents of the dynasty did not, however, yield without a struggle. The seat of authority was removed south to Parandá, and later on to Junnar, and a new ruler, descended from the old Nizámsháhi stock, was placed on the throne, and in his name, Malikambar governed the kingdom and led the Deccan armies and retook Ahmednagar, and kept at bay the Moghuls and their allies, the Bijápur Adilsháhi kings for twenty years and more.

In the long and arduous struggle, which Malikambar waged with the Moghuls, Shaháji, the father of Shiváji, the Nimbálkar Náiks of Faltan, and the great Lakhoji Jádhavráo, fought on the side of the Ahmednagar kings, and though defeated in 1620, the defeat was due to the misconduct of the Mahomedan nobles while the Maráthá soldiers and leaders fought with distinction. Lakhoji Jádhavráo, indeed, went over to the Moghuls, who in 1621 conferred upon him command of 15,000 horse and 2,000 foot, and Malikambar himself was compelled soon after to give up Ahmednagar, and surrender the new ruler he had set up twenty years before. He rallied his forces even after this great blow, but his premature death in 1626 removed the only man who could gather round him the resisting power of the country, and lead it to success. Even

Shaháji Bhonslé, at one time, broke off his connection with the hopeless Nizámsháhi ruler, and he received a command of 5,000 horse from the Moghul Emperor. The Nizám was murdered by his minister, the son of Malikambar, in 1631. Just when the condition of affairs looked most desperate, Shaháji Bhonslé again came to the rescue of his old masters, and proclaimed another successor to the throne of the Nizámsháhis. He established his authority over the Konkan and over the Désh from the Nirá river to the Chándore hills, and the Moghul Emperor had to send an army of 25,000 men to dislodge Shaháji from place to place. The struggle was maintained for four years, 1632—1636, but the odds were too great, and Shaháji had to yield at last before the superior forces of Shahájahán, and with the Emperor's consent, entered the service of the Bijápur Kings in 1637.

The Ahmednagar territories thus conquered were formed into the new *Subhá* of Aurangábád, and embraced parts of Násik and Khándésh, the whole of the Bérárs, and a part of Northern Konkan. The remaining portions of the kingdom, especially the country between the Bhimá and the

Nirá, fell to the share of the Bijápur kings. The Moghuls now turned their arms against the Adilsháhi rulers of Bijápur who had helped them in the destruction of Ahmednagar. The first formal treaty between the two powers was formed in 1601, and the friendship was cemented by a marriage alliance. These were only temporary obstacles in the way. Ibráhim Adilsháh, the greatest of the Bijápur monarchs, died in 1626, and his successor Mahmed Adilsháh had to defend his city against the armies of the Moghuls, who laid seige in 1631, and again in 1636, till at last he had to make peace with the Moghuls. He agreed to pay twenty lacs as tribute to the Delhi Emperor and to give up Shaháji, who was still supporting the desperate cause of the Nizámsháhi Kings. Shaháji soon after entered the Bijápur service and was sent to the Karnátik, where he made important conquests and carved out a kingdom in the Kávéri valley for one of his sons. The Mahomedan principalities of Bérár and Bédar had already been dismembered and their territories absorbed in the kingdoms of Bijápur and Ahmednagar. Golcondá alone remained nominally independent, but it saved itself this time by consenting to pay tribute to Shahájahán. The Moghuls levied a heavy war-tribute which the ruler was wholly unable to pay, but he had to submit to it, as his capital, Hyderábád, had been taken by surprise by Shahájahán's son, Aurangzéb, and he was shut up in the fort of Golcondá.

The Portuguese power also, which was so formidable in the sixteenth century, had spent itself, and was now acting on the defensive on the coast line of the Konkan, while the English Company had just established a factory at Surat and commanded no political importance.

The predominant factor in the political situation about the time that Shivāji was born and during the period of his boyhood was thus the advance of the Moghul arms in the South. The Deccan powers had been unable to make head against this overwhelming force which came with all the prestige which had helped the Emperors to cement together a vast empire spreading from Kábul to the Bay of Bengal and the hills of Kámun to the heart of the Deccan. The conditions of Alá-ud-din's invasion of 1216 were thus repeating themselves after three hundred years with a momentum which made resistance hopeless.

The Hindus had then yielded to the avalanche which swept over the land. They had, however, learned wisdom under the hard discipline of subjection to their foreign Afghán and Turkish masters. They had been able to turn aside the edge of foreign conquest and had even succeeded in taming the violence of the foreigners. Their own vernacular had become the language of the Court and the *Darbár.*

The revenue management of the country was entirely in their own hands. Their Military Commanders had distinguished themselves on the battle-fields, and their Ministers in the Council Chambers. Murárào and Shaháji Bhonslé had become the chief supports of the authority of the Bijápur rulers. Madan Pandit was in power at Golcondá. The western *ghâts* and hill-forts and the Mávals were in the hands of their great nobles. Chandrarào Moré was in charge of the Ghátmáthá from the sources of the Krishná to the Wárná. The Sávants were in charge of Southern Konkan, the Nimbálkars were in power in Faltan and the Daflés and Mánés in the Eastern Sátárá regions. The Bhonslés were in charge of the Pooná Mávals and their *jahágir* extended as far east as Báràmati and Indápur.

The Ghorpadés and Ghádgés, the Mahádiks, the Mohités, and Mámulkars were similarly in the command of considerable horse and foot. The most reliable, if not the chief fighting men, in the Golcondá, Bijápur and Ahmednagar armies had been men of the Maráthá race who had measured strength with the heavily armed soldiers of the North, and had realized their strength and weakness. Under these circumstances when the new Moghul invasion threatened the land, it was but natural that new thoughts should surge up in the minds of many, the like of which had not troubled their ancestors three centuries before. Those three centuries had left lasting memories of past horrors, and justified apprehensions of the renewal of the fanatical intolerance and cruelty which the Mahomedan conquerors, left to themselves, were so prone to exhibit in their dealings with the people of the country. Those three centuries had also witnessed a revival of the religious spirit among the Hindu population. Colonel Wilkes in his "History of Mysore" speaks of a prophesy which he found recorded in a Hindu manuscript of 1646 in the Mackenzie collection, in which the prophet after describing "the ruin of all virtue and religion, and the humiliation which the noblest in the land had been made to suffer," concludes with a hope that "the time for deliverance will come at last, and the virgins will announce it with songs of joy, and the skies will shower their flowers." This prophecy was written in Southern India at a time when Shiváji's name was not known beyond his *jahágir* in Pooná, but Colonel Wilkes testifies that the application of it was by universal agreement made to the deliverance which Rájá Shiváji was the instrument of effecting by his genius and his arms before the century had far advanced.

While the Musalman chroniclers denounced Shiváji as a *galim* or free-booter, the writers of native *Bakhars* or chronicles, true to the ancient *Puránic* ideal, ascribed this deliverance to the Earth in form of a cow supplicating help from above, and the god of gods promising to come to the relief of his oppressed worshippers in the shape of a new incarnation. It is in the spirit of the same fond superstition that native historians trace for Shiváji a fabled descent from the royal house of Udépur. Shiváji was neither a robber nor an incarnation, nor did he derive his strength from his supposed Rajput descent. He was nobly born in being Shaháji's and

Jijái's son, and nobly connected in that his mother was a daughter of Lakhoji Jádhavráo, and his wife, daughter of the famous Jagdevráo Náik Nimbálkar. To be born of such a father and mother was a privilege of greater value than any that legend or fable could confer on young Shiváji. He was a man whose strength lay in his realizing in his person the best aspirations of the age and the race to which he belonged. Such men are not born without long preparation nor out of their time or in a country where the popular mind has not been educated to appreciate and support them.

The impulse which animated men to take a more hopeful view of the situation was not the result of mere secular or calculating prudence. Such prudence was well personified in the old tutor to whom Shiváji's education and training had been consigned by his father. He represented the past while the heart of the young boy under his charge was bursting with the hopes of a brighter future. Prudence was well represented in his grandfather Lakhoji Jádhavráo and his father Shaháji, who transferred their services from state to state and turned their faces from the setting to the rising sun and felt no higher faith in them. All accounts agree in describing Shiváji from his early youth as being intensely fond of hearing the old epics of *Rámáyan* and *Mahábhárat.* He would walk many miles to attend a *Kathá* or recital of them by specially noted preachers. Shiváji's mind was cast in an intensely religious mould, and he continued to be, above all, religious throughout his chequered career. This revived feeling of confidence in other possibilities than those which his prudent teacher and his near relation realized for him sprung from this religious source. Shiváji felt in him what religious enthusiasm alone can inspire, the feeling that he had a commission which required him to think little of his own interests and advancement. Of course, he did not himself realize the full force of this enthusiasm in his earlier years. There was a good deal of the wild-oats sowing in his earlier exploits, but the sense that he had a mission to achieve grew with him every day of his life. It is recorded that on three memorable occasions he was determined to give up all his possessions and retire from worldly life to seek salvation, and on all these occasions it was with great difficulty that his teachers and ministers prevailed on him to entertain more correct notions of his duty in life. Throughout his career on all occasions of great trial, when the times were so critical that a single false step would prove the ruin of all his hopes, he resigned himself to prayer and asked for a sign and awaited in expectation the manifestation of a higher voice speaking through him when he was beside himself in a fit of possession. The ministers were made to write down the reply so vouchsafed for their master's information, and Shiváji acted upon it with implicit faith, whether that voice told him to make his peace with Aurangzéb and go to Delhi to be a prisoner of his enemies or to meet Afzulkhán single-handed in a possibly mortal combat. These stories of self-resignation and self-possession distinctly point out and emphasize the fact that it was not merely secular consideration or deep policy which governed his motions. The impulse came from a higher part of our common or rather uncommon nature.

Foreign writers of Indian history have not been able to understand this feature in Shiváji's character, although more than his hardihood and enterprise, it was this mental characteristic which made him a representative man of the age. The only motive power which is strong enough to move the masses in this country is an appeal to their religious faith. During the past three hundred years the whole of India had been visibly moved by the new contact with the Mahomedan militant creed, and there had been action and reaction of a very marked kind. The rise of the *Vaishnav* sects represented by the followers of Rámánuja, Rámánand, and other Puritan teachers had made men feel that salvation was a concern for all, and that before God's throne there was no difference between the high-born and the low. This teaching is the most distinct mark of the doctrines of Rámánand, of Kabir, of Rámdás, Rohidás, Surdás, Nának, and Chaitanya, who flourished in different parts of Northern and Eastern India. The severity of the monotheistic creed of the Mahomedans was distinctly impressed upon the minds of some of these prophets. The worshippers of Dattátraya or the incarnation of the Hindu Trinity, often clothed their God in the garb of a Mahomedan *Fakir.* This same influence was at work with greater effect on the popular mind in Maháráshtra, where preachers, both Bráhmans and non-Bráhmans, were calling on people to identify Rám with Rahim, and ensure their freedom from the bonds of formal ritualism and caste distinctions and unite in common love of man and faith in one God. Contemporaneously with the political leaders, Tukárám, Rámdás, Eknáth, and Jayarámswámi were the religious leaders of this movement, which was, moreover, not confined to the higher castes, but claimed representatives from all classes, high and low. The cult of Vithobá, the traditions of Pandharpur, the heaven on earth, attracted thousands every year, and the extempore recitals or *Kathás* drew thousands more in every town and village. The effect of these lectures was best exemplified in the counsel which Rájá Sawái Jayasingh gave to his master Aurangzéb in 1678, when the *Jezziah* or Hindu poll-tax, abolished by Akbar, was re-imposed. He reminded his master that "God was not the God of Mahomedans alone, but he was the God of all mankind. The Pagan and the Moslem stand alike before Him. To nullify the religious customs of Hindus is to set at naught the will of the Almighty." This was a new feeling, and it yet represented the general consensus of the people. The Mahomedans themselves had learned to feel the force of this higher teaching. Abul Fazil and Faizi had translated *Mahábhárat* and *Rámáyan* in the same spirit. Akbar strived with a singular devotion to amalgamate the two religions in a new dispensation which was intended to abolish all religious differences. Prince Dárá-shéko, the eldest son of Shahájahán, translated the *Upanishads* and the *Gitá*, and represented these aspirations of enlightened Mahomedans, and it was on this account, as much as for his birthright, that Aurangzéb made war on him, and hunted him to death. Mahomedan saints like Kabir in the north and Shaik Mahomed in Maháráshtra preached the same higher law to Hindus and Mahomedans alike, and though worshipped after death by both communities, they were disregarded by bigots of both creeds in their lifetime.

This then was the situation. Religious revival and a Puritan enthusiasm were at work in the land, and it was clear to men's minds that the old bigotry must cease. This religious enlightenment was the principal point of departure from the earlier traditions of submission to brute force, and it made itself manifest in the form of a determination that Mahomedan intolerance should not again overspread the land. None felt this influence more strongly than the worshippers, who placed their faith in the shrines of Bhawáni at Tuljápur and Kolhápur. They caught this fire, and communicated it to others through their bards, the *Gondhlis* and the *Bháts.*

Shivâji, who mixed on equal terms with Tukárám, Rámdás, and other religious teachers of his time, represented these new aspirations in an intensified form in his own proper person. This was one chief source of his strength and his hold on the people, and it represented a strength which no prudent calculations of chances could ever confer.

Another influence which operated on Shivâji's mind with a force not realized by his father or teacher was the feeling that the threatened invasion of the foreign Moslem conquerors could only be adequately met by an united opposition. Shivâji's teacher Rámdás tersely put this conception of Shivâji's aims and policy in his verses of advice, communicated to his unfortunate son Sambháji, to unite all who were Maráthás, and propagate the duty or *dharma* of a great *ráshtra* or united nation. This was the whole end and aim of Shivâji's policy, and it explains some of his more questionable acts. He felt that the Moghul would surely prevail, just as the Afghan had done three hundred years before, if the nobles of the land quarrelled among themselves and fought with each other—each striving only to keep or increase his own little *Jahágir* or *Vatan* intact at the cost of his neighbour. The times dictated a policy of union and mutual trust for a common purpose. Everybody, whether Hindu or Mahomedan, who came in the way of the realization of this idea, had to be put down, whether he was a friend or foe, a relation or a stranger.

This weakness of internal dissensions is an ever-present danger in all times and phases of Indian history. It has been happily described as the tendency to be unorganised and centrifugal, to resent discipline and subordination. No wonder that such unorganized power cannot maintain itself against organised force or skill arrayed against it, in the battle-field or in the Council Hall. In the smaller arrangements as well as in his larger schemes, Shiváji tried to interlace men's interests or ambitions in a way to make them feel pride in common success and shame in common defeat. The Ghádgés, the Morés, and the Ghorpadés represented this separatist tendency, and they had to be disposed of by superior force or skill, before the leading

Maráthá families accepted the higher trust Shiváji reposed in them. The Mahomedan powers themselves had to be played one against the other in the pursuit of the same end and, though at times Shiváji had to yield to superior force, yet throughout his career, this desire of union against the foreigner remained a predominant factor in his mind. It is true, even Shiváji failed at times, and it is certain his attempts failed at last, but it was a noble failure which failed after the structure he had built up was able to sustain shocks of a kind which had toppled down more ambitious piles.

One other feature may be noticed here before we are done with this delineation of the way in which the seed of life was sown in a soil prepared by the hard discipline of centuries to receive it. Shiváji had the magnetic power which only true leaders of men possess, and which neither bandits nor mad fanatics can ever claim. He attracted towards himself all that was hopeful and aspiring in the land, without distinction of class or caste or creed or colour. His very councillors were selected from all the great communities which constituted the strength of the country. His touch made the very grossest of men feel a cleansing fire burning within them. The Mávlis and the Hétkaris did not follow him solely for the booty they acquired, and when they could no longer help him in distant expeditions, Shiváji did not fail to employ Musalmans both on sea and land to carry out his designs. Tánáji Málusaré and his brother Suryáji, Báji Fasalkar and Nétáji Pálkar, the Prabhus Báji Déshpándé and Báláji Ávaji, the Bráhmans Moropant, Ábáji Sondév, Raghunáth Náráyan, Ánnáji Datto, Janárdanpant Hanmanté, the Maráthás Pratápráo Gujar and Hambirrao Mohité, Santáji Ghorpadé and Dhanáji Jádhav, the ancestors of Parsoji Bhonslé, and Udáji Pavár, and Khandéráo Dábhádé, all served under him in his armies and none proved faithless to him. This is the highest privilege of genius. These men stuck to their posts even when Shiváji was a captive at Delhi and helped him to establish his power without an effort when he escaped and returned back to his country. Later on, when, after his death, his son Sambháji misbehaved and was killed, and Sháhu was led a captive from Ráigad, these same men and their successors bore the brunt of the Moghul conquest, and though compelled to retire to the south, only did so, to return with renewed strength to complete the discomfiture of Aurangzéb at the total failure of his ambitious schemes.

Lastly, Shivâji's self-discipline was as great as his power of control and his military daring. This characteristic of his nature stands out in marked contrast with the looseness and ferocity of those times. In the worst excesses committed by his armies under the stress of war and need of money, cows, women, and cultivators were never molested. Women especially were treated with a chivalry unknown to his enemies. When captured in the chances of war, they were sent back to their husbands with all honours. He saw the danger of making assignments in *jahágirs* of conquered lands and set his face against the proposal made to him. His successors did not observe this caution of their master and accelerated the dismemberment of the Empire, whose foundation he had laid with such wisdom.

Religious fervour, almost at white heat, bordering on the verge of self-abnegation, a daring and adventurous spirit born of a confidence that a higher power than man's protected him and his work, the magnetism of superior genius, which binds men together and leads them to victory, a rare insigh into the real needs of the times, and a steadfastness of purpose, which no adverse turn of fortune could conquer, a readiness and resourcefulness rarely met with either in European or Indian history, true patriotism, which was far in advance of the times and a sense of justice tempered with mercy,—these were the sources of the strength that enabled Shiváji to sow the seeds of a power which accomplished in the hands of his successors all that he had planned out, and enabled his race to write a chapter in Indian history to some purpose. With the thread furnished by this preliminary examination of the character of the founder of the Maráthá Empire, we shall now be better able to follow the labyrinth of the story of his life, and sit in judgment upon the more particular events of his singularly noble career.

CHAPTER IV.

HOW THE SEED THRIVED.

SHIVAJI'S FELLOW-WORKERS.

THE short sketch we attempted to delineate in the preceding chapter will present to the reader's mind the leading characteristics of the great Captain who gathered together the scattered forces of Maráthá power, and under the protecting shadows of the strong hill-forts of Western India, bound them together into a great kingdom, with larger potentialities before it in the near future. It is however obvious that the work of liberation, on which Shiváji had set his heart, was a work in which he required co-operation. The seed sown by him could only sprout and thrive in a suitable soil. If the leading spirits of the times had not been prepared by a long and arduous discipline to co-operate with him, even Shiváji's towering genius would have failed to accomplish the great task he had undertaken. Both Native and European writers of Máráthá history have been so taken up with the absorbing interest of the history of Shiváji's life that they have often lost sight of the fact that he only represented in a higher degree the gifts of body and mind and the aspiring ambition of the men of his times, and that success became possible to him only because the seed he sowed was watered by capable men in all ranks of life, who accepted him as their captain and leader. He was eminently *primus in pares*, and never regarded himself in any other light. We propose in this chapter to give a running sketch of the fellow-workers of Shiváji, the soldiers and statesmen, and the spiritual teachers, who rose about this time to eminence. The materials to hand for such life-sketches are but poor, but the moral of this story will be hardly understood till we reproduce even dimly on the canvas of history a reflex of the features of those great and heroic men, whose influence shaped the story of Shiváji's life, and whose memories are still our best inheritance.

The first place in this historic picture of the past, must be assigned to Jijábái, the mother of Shiváji. She claimed a descent from the ancient Yádav kings of Mahárashtra and was the daughter of the proudest

Maráthá *Jahágirdár* of the times. The story of her romantic marriage with Shaháji, when they were both children, is eminently typical of the times. Her father in an unguarded moment expressed a wish that she should be Shaháji's wife, and the pledge was enforced by Shaháji's father, Máloji Ráj́é, by a sacrilege which at once showed that Máloji was a man who could hold his own against even the great Jádhavráo, commander of twenty thousand horse. If Jádhavráo claimed his descent from the Yádav Kings of Dévgiri, Shaháji traced his lineage back to the Rajput princes of Udépur. Well-born and well-connected as she was, Jijábái was greater still in the heroism which ennobles men and women in the humblest circumstances of life. Her father never excused the injury that had mortified his pride, and the turn of events, which made Shaháji king-maker at Ahmednagar and Daulatábád, only aggravated this enmity. Jádhavráo went over to the Moghul invaders, and Shaháji was forced to give up the defence of the Ahmednagar kings. He retired to Bijápur hotly pursued by his father-in-law, leaving his wife behind him, a fugitive and a captive in the hands of her father. In these adverse circumstances, Jijábái was left to her own resources, about the time that she gave birth to the great Shiváji in the fort of Shivanér. Jijábái, abandoned by her father and husband, had good reason to feel in her own person the indignity of foreign subjection. In her desolate condition young Shiváji was all in all to her, and she brought him up relying solely on the protection of the gods, especially the Goddess Bhawáni, who had spared her and her child in the midst of such afflictions. Later on, with Shaháji's permission, she removed to his *jahágir* at Pooná, then managed by Dádoji Kondadev, Shaháji's trusted minister. The hill forts which surrounded the place were associated in Shiváji's memories as his only safe home, and no wonder that, with such a mother, and with such associations, he developed a character of hardihood and enterprise from his earliest days. The boy loved his mother with an affection which had no bounds. His father never lived with him but his mother was always at hand. Throughout his life, she was the guiding genius and protecting deity whose approbation rewarded all toil and filled him with a courage which nothing could daunt. The religious turn of mind, and the strong faith in his mission, so prominent in his character, Shiváji owed entirely to his mother, who literally fed him on the old *Puránic* legends of bravery and war. When on Shaháji's death, Jijábái desired to immolate herself, it was Shiváji's entreaties which reconciled her to live with him a little while longer. Shiváji left his kingdom in her charge when he went to Delhi, and in all the great crises of his life he first invoked her blessings, and she always charged him to attempt the most hazardous feats, trusting in divine protection. If ever great men owed their greatness to the inspiration of their mothers, the influence of Jijábái was a factor of prime importance in the making of Shiváji's career, and the chief source of his strength.

Next only to Jijábái's influence over young Shiváji, must rank the part played by Dádoji Kondadev who stood in Shaháji's place as guardian of the child and the administrator of his father's estates. Dádoji was born in Málthán in the Pooná district, and had seen much service. All the care and affection which Shaháji, if he had been near, might have bestowed upon the young child in his tender years, were ungrudgingly shown by Dádoji in the bringing up of his ward to fulfil his great destinies. By disposition, he was cautious to a degree which made it difficult for him at times to sympathise with the wild freedom with which Shiváji loved to roam over the hills, but his love for his charge was unstinted, and at last he was persuaded that Shiváji was not to be judged by the ordinary standards of men, and that the ideas over which the young man brooded were of a sort in which even failure was glorious. Shiváji's wildness needed the curb and the guidance of a strict disciplinarian like the old master under whose care he was brought up. He taught the young boy all the arts of peace and war which it was good for him to know; and he taught him what was more valuable still, the way to organise and control undisciplined forces. Dádoji was a masterhand in the art of civil government. Before he took over the charge of the *jahágir*, it had been much devastated by the famine and border wars between the Moghuls and the Bijápur kings. Pooná itself had been depopulated; packs of wolves, and bands of robbers, fiercer than wolves, made husbandry impossible. In the course of a few years, Dádoji destroyed the wolves by offering rewards and he destroyed the robber-bands by stern repression. Long and favourable leases were granted to the settlers who agreed to cultivate the soil, and before ten years had passed, Dádoji was able to show to his master that the estate was in a flourishing condition which enabled him to employ a large number of foot-soldiers and burghers, and keep the hill-forts repaired and garrisoned. Pooná and Supá, Indápur and Bárámati, with the Mávals, thus enjoyed the blessings of peace and well-ordered control. Plantations of fruit-trees smiled over the land, and still bear testimony at Shivápur to the wisdom of the great Bráhman-minister. So strict was his discipline that once when he was tempted to pluck without leave a ripe mango of one of his master's trees, he ordered those about him to cut off his right hand by way of self-inflicted punishment. The entreaties of his followers were allowed to prevail and the hand was spared, but he ceased to wear the sleeve on the right side as a token of the unconscious wrong he had done, till Shaháji ordered him to discontinue the practice. Of course, Dádoji's ambition was of the old school, to make Shiváji a partisan leader like his father and grandfather. He could not, till his last moments, rise to the height of the thoughts over which Shiváji's mind was brooding, to unite these partisan leaders, and effect their common liberation from the Moslem yoke. When, however, he was satisfied that his young charge had the capacity to realise this wild dream, the old man yielded and blessed him before he died. Shiváji's revenue system and his civil government were entirely modelled upon the practice of his teacher, Dádoji, and it is not too much to say, that, without such a guiding hand to regulate and curb his wildness, the success which attended Shiváji would not have been so certain and permanent as it proved in the end.

Dádoji's death occurred just when Shiváji first launched his fortunes upon a career of adventure and peril by seizing Torná, and fortifying Ráigad. During the ten years that he had administered the estate, Dádoji had trained a number of Bráhman *kárkoons* in the service to supply his place, in the extended fields of operation upon which Shiváji had now entered. Ábáji Sondév, Raghunáth Ballál, Shámarájpant, and the elder Pinglé, father of Moropant, and Nárcpant Hanmanté, were all trained in this school both as civil officers and military commanders. These men sympathised with their young master's spirit of adventure, and they and other kindred spirits, Moropant

Pinglé, Annáji Datto, Niráji Pandit, Ráoji Somnáth, Dattáji Gopináth, Raghunáthpant, and Gangáji Mangáji, proved of eminent service to him in his ambitious plans. They represented the brain of the new movement. The iron hand and the heart of steel which alone could ensure its success were also ready to hand in the Mávli leaders who were Shiváji's chosen companions in boyhood. Three such are specially mentioned in the histories, Yésáji Kank, Tánáji Málusaré, and Báji Fasalkar, who were all men brought up in the hard discipline of their mountain hill-forts. Firangoji Narasálé, Sambháji Káwji, Mánkoji Dahátondé, Gomáji Náik, Nétáji Pálkar, Suryáji Málusaré, Hiroji Farjand, Dévji Gádhwé, and others also belong to the same Mávli stock. They were soon joined by the great Prabhu leaders, Murár Báji Prabhu of Mahád, and Báji Prabhu of Hirdas Mával, and Báláji Ávji Chitnis from the Habshi territories. The two Bájis had been in the service of Shiváji's enemies, and were taken over by him in his service for their gallantry. There was such a charm about Shiváji's personality that even those who were his enemies, and whom he had conquered on the battle-field, became his trusted followers. The Bráhmans, the Prabhus, and the Mávli leaders were the chief sources of Shiváji's strength in these earlier years. The representatives of the great Maráthá families in the service of Bijápur and Ahmednagar, so far from helping the movement, proved to be its most bitter foes. Báji Mohité, a relation of Shaháji, had to be surprised at Supá and sent away to the Karnátik.

Báji Ghorpadé of Mudhol was mean enough to entrap Shaháji at the bidding of the king of Bijápur, and Shiváji had to suppress him by terrible revenge. The Morés of Jávli allowed a Bráhman emissary from Bijápur to hide in their territory, with a view to assassinate Shiváji, and the Morés had to be disposed of in self-defence by arts which were inexcusable under any other circumstances. The Sávants of Wádi and the Dalvis of the Konkan and the Shirkés and Survés of Shringárpur were similarly obstructive, and refused to join the new movement, and they had therefore to be suppressed, or, as in the case of Sávants, subordinated to the new power. The Nimbálkars of Faltan, and Mánés of Mhaswad and Zunjárráo Ghádgé, all in the Bijápur service, continued to fight against the national movement which Shiváji had undertaken to organise, and remained true to their old allegiance. It will be thus seen that the strength of the new movement lay entirely in the middle-classes of the population, the old Maráthá *Jahágirdár* families contributing little or no help till at a later stage. When, however, the first difficulties were overcome, the new generation of young men, belonging to the highest families entered Shiváji's service and became his most trusted leaders. Pratápráo Gujar, Hambirráo Mohité, Shidoji Nimbálkar, Sambháji Moré, Suryaráo Kákadé, Santáji Ghorpadé, Dhanáji Jádhav, Khandéráo Dábhádé, Parsoji and Rupáji Bhonslé and Nemáji Shindé are all names which figured in the later history of Shiváji's life, and they soon succeeded in securing to the movement the support, not only of the middle and lower classes, but of the best and most aristocratic families in the country. This is a point of some importance to note, for it shows clearly that the movement was initiated by the people and by their natural leaders, who only joined it when the success became assured.

Even the Mahomedans felt the influence that was at work. Shiváji's chief admiral, Daryá Surung, was a Mahomedan, and fought with the Siddi admirals of the Moghuls, so was Ibráhimkhán, a *pathán* leader, a Mahomedan. The disbanded Mahomedan soldiery and troopers from Bijápur and Golcondá entered Shiváji's service, and were with some misgivings admitted into separate corps.

The relative importance of the Bráhman and the Prabhu elements on one side, and the Mávli and Maráthá elements on the other, will be fully realised from the fact, that in Grant Duff's history the names of twenty Bráhman leaders and four Prabhus are mentioned as against twenty Mávli and Maráthá leaders. These Mávlis and Maráthás were opposed to about fourteen Maráthá partizan leaders in the Bijápur and Moghul service. All the Bráhman Ministers, except the *Panditráo* and the *Nyáyádhish*, had in those days of trouble to be military commanders as well as civil officers, and they discharged this double function with equal credit. The Native *Bakhars* make mention of twice as many names, but the relative proportions shown above are not much disturbed. There are about fifty Bráhman and Prabhu leaders mentioned as against forty Mávli and Maráthá leaders in the narrative of Chitnis's great *Bakhar*, though in the final list given at the end of the work forty-five Bráhman and seventy-five Mávli and Maráthá names are mentioned. Roughly speaking about a hundred men from all classes of society thus came to prominence, and were the chief supports of the new Hindu dynasty that was established at Ráigad, in opposition to the Moslem powers. We can only here select a few of these men whose deeds have been sung by national bards, or chronicled in the records of the time, but they will be typical of the rest who, in their own humbler places, performed feats of valour and devotion, which contributed equally to the success of the common cause.

Among the Bráhman leaders, the Hanmantés, both father and sons, naturally occupied the first place. Náropant Hanmanté was, like Dádoji Kondadév in Shaháji's service, having charge of his Karnátik possessions. His sons, Raghunáth Náráyan and Janárdanpant, were worthy of their father. Raghunáthpant helped to carve out for Shaháji's other son Vénkoji a new kingdom at Tanjore, and when differences arose between him and his master, Raghunáthpant retired to the fortress of Gingi, and held that station as also a portion of Arcot, and

Véllore, and several strong posts in Mysore, till Shiváji, at his request, made his final expedition into the Karnátik and the Dravid country. The importance of these possessions in the south was fully realised when Aurangzéb captured Sambháji, and conquered the hill-forts one by one, and the Maráthá leaders had to retreat to the south at Gingi, whence they returned in a few years back to their country, and forced Aurangzéb in his turn to admit his discomfiture. Raghunáthpant's brother Janárdanpant served under Shiváji in the later wars with the Moghuls. Such were these Hanmantés, men of iron courage, and at the same time great in the wisdom of their counsels.

Moropant Pinglé may well be described as the chief pillar of Shiváji's power, and earned his *Péshwáship* by distinguished services in extending the conquests in Northern Konkan and Báglan. He was a great builder of forts, and a great organizer of Shiváji's armies. His father was in Shaháji's service in the Karnátik, but Moropant returned home when still a youth and joined Shiváji's army in 1653. The first *Péshwá*, Shámarájpant, failed to achieve success in the wars in the Konkan with the

Siddis and the Sávants, and Moropant was sent by his master to retrieve the loss, and succeeded in his mission. He was constantly engaged in all the wars of those times, and outlived his master only a short time. The *Péshwáship* survived in his family till Sháhu bestowed it upon Báláji Vishvanáth in 1714. He was Shivájí's chief civil adviser, as also his principal military commander, and there was no man at the time who could be mentioned as more capable and more devoted to the national interest.

Ábáji Sondév was trained in the same school with the Hanmantés and the Pinglés. He was the first to go outside the *Jahágir* limits, and take the offensive by attacking Kalyán which, though retaken several times by the Moghuls, continued to be an advanced Maráthá outpost in Ábáji Sondév's charge, as *Subhédár* in the Konkan. He was also, like Moropant, a great builder of forts. When Shiváji went to Delhi, Abáji and Moropant were left in charge of the kingdom as advisers of Jijábái. He was first appointed *Muzumdár* and his son was appointed *Amátya* at the time of the coronation.

Rágho Ballál Atré distinguished himself in the wars with the Siddis. He took prominent part in the suppression of Chandraráo Moré, and it was his chief distinction that the first *Pathán* soldiers employed by Shiváji were placed under his command.

Annáji Datto was another Bráhman leader who rose to be *Surnis* and *Pantasachiv* in Shiváji's time. He took an active part in the conquest of Panhálá and Ránganá, and in the Konkan wars, and led the first expedition in the Karnátik, when he plundered, Hubli. He had the charge of South Konkan just as Ábáji Sondév and Moropant had the charge of North Konkan and Báglan. He was associated with these commanders in the charge of the Maráthá territory, when Shiváji went to Delhi.

Dattáji Gopináth was *Wáknis* and *Mantri*, in charge of Shiváji's household affairs, and served Shiváji in the important mission to Afzulkhán. The famous Sakhárám Bápu Bokil of later Maráthá history was descended from this family.

Ráoji Somnáth was in charge of the Bérár conquests, and served in the Konkan wars also. His father Somnáth was *Dabir* and foreign minister, and was succeeded by Janárdanpant Hanmante in those posts.

Niráji Ráoji was *Nyáyádhish* and his son Pralhád was ambassador at Golcondá and in Ráját́m's time became *Pratinidhi*, in consequence of his great talents in organising the defence of Gingi.

Among the Prabhu Commanders and Councillors, the principal names are Murár Báji, Báji Prabhu, and Báláji Ávji.

Murár Báji was in charge of Purandar fort, and defended it against the attacks of Dilérkhan with great heroism, and at the cost of his life.

Báji Prabhu, from being an enemy, was converted into a devoted follower. When Shiváji escaped from Panhálá and went to Ránganá, he posted himself with a thousand men in a narrow defile, where he contested every inch of ground with the Bijápur General, in command of overwhelming forces, till he heard the gun announcing Shiváji's safe arrival at Ránganá, when at last he gave up breath, exhausted from the effects of the wounds he had received. This exploit and sacrifice have been compared by some with the heroic defence of the Pass at Thermopylæ, so well known to the readers of Greek history.

Báláji Ávji was descended from a noble family in the Habshi's service, and like Báláji Vishvanáth later on, was forced to leave his native village to save his life. He attracted Shiváji's notice in 1648 by his cleverness, and continued to be the chief secretary throughout Shiváji's life. His son and grandson also played an important part in the two succeeding reigns, and one of his descendants wrote the great chronicle, known as the Chitnis's *Bakhar*.

Among the Mávli Commanders, Yésáji Kank was the chief of the Mávli infantry, and did important service in the earlier conquests. He and Tánáji continued to be Shiváji's chief associates all through their life. They were both with him when Afzulkhán was killed, as also when Sháhistékhán was assaulted in his own palace, and they both accompanied Shiváji to Delhi.

Tánáji Málusaré and his brother Suryáji are names immortalised by native bards for the courage they showed in escalading

Sinhagad, where Tánáji met his death, and Suryáji took his revenge upon the garrison.

Báji Fasalkar Déshmukh met his death in a combat with the Sávants in the Konkan wars. Firangoji Narasálé was the Commander of the Chákan fort, and made it over to Shiváji in 1648. He was one of those who, though once an enemy, became a trusted friend, and when the Moghul reconquered Chákan, and tempted him by an offer of service, he refused the temptation and joined Shiváji's army.

Sambháji Káwji with Raghunáthpant took part in the attack on Jávli when Chandraráo Moré was killed. While Yésáji Kank was the Commander of the Mávli infantry, Nétáji Pálkar was the Commander of the cavalry. He was the most dashing officer in the army, and extended Shiváji's plundering expeditions to the east as far as Ahmednagar, Jálná and Aurangábád. He was here, there and everywhere, wherever danger was to be faced.

The next Commander of the Cavalry was Pratápráo Gujar, and he worthily sustained the confidence his master placed in him in defeating the Moghul armies in Báglan, and the Bijápur armies near Panhálá. He was in charge of the Maráthá forces stationed at Aurangábád, during the two years of peace between Shiváji and the Emperor. Having failed in keeping up a hot pursuit of the Bijápur forces, he was censured by Shiváji, and on the next occasion when he encountered the enemy, he achieved a complete victory with the loss of his own life like Tánáji Malusaré, and Báji Prabhu, and Báji Fasalkar, and Suryaráo Kákadé.

Among the younger generals, Khandéráo Dábhádé, Parsoji Bhonslé, Santáji Ghorpadé and Dhanáji Jádhav, became well-known names in the generation subsequent to Shiváji's death. The first two laid the foundations of Maráthá power in Gujarát and Bérár, while the last two brought the war of independence to a successful issue.

Such were the men whose prowess and counsel helped Shiváji to found the kingdom. Not one of them failed in doing his duty in the hour of danger, not one proved treacherous to his master, or went over to the enemy, while many died at their posts in the hour of victory, consoled with the thought that they had done service assigned to them. These are facts, which redound to their credit, as well as the love Shiváji inspired in them towards his person, and the cause he laboured to promote. The kingdom founded by labours and sacrifices, such as these, included at the time of his coronation, 1674, not only the hereditary *Jahágir* about Pooná, Supá, Indápur and Bárámati, but all the Mávals, the western parts of the Sátárá district up to Wái, Sátárá and Karád, the western portions of Kolhápur, south and north Konkan, including the sea fortresses and the hill fortresses, Báglan, and posts in Karnátik, Vélloré, Bédnore and Mysore. All these territories passed from the hands of Shiváji's successor and became Moghul conquests within a few years after Shiváji's death. The permanent acquisition made was thus not so much of territory and treasure as the higher acquisition of self-confidence and union among the Maráthá leaders, the spirit which taught the Maráthá race that it was possible to resist successfully the inroads of Mahomedan powers. It was this spirit which proved the salvation of the country during the twenty-two years that Aurangzéb spent in the conquest of the Deccan from 1685 to 1707. If it had not been for the schooling and discipline which the leaders of the nation, civil and military, had obtained during the successful wars waged by Shiváji against his enemies, no such result would have been possible. These hundred men, so brought up and disciplined, inspired the nation with a new hope and a new courage which helped them to feel unabated confidence in their powers of resistance, and in the ultimate success of their efforts to turn back the tide which threatened to overwhelm. It is on this account that we have deemed it necessary to devote an entire chapter to sketch the careers of the more notable leaders, the memories of whose deeds inspired their successors to follow in their footsteps. Shiváji by his great personality filled the rank and file of his followers with his own spirit, and this was the mission of his life. His territories and his treasures passed away from the feeble hands of his son, but the spirit he had inspired in his men remained untamed by reverses, and only gathered new strength, as the odds against them increased. Before a much smaller army, led by Jayasingh and Dilérkhán, Shiváji found it politic to tender his submission and go to Delhi. His successors had to face the whole brunt of the Moghul forces led by the Emperor in person, and though they had to retreat to the south, they offered no submission, but returned home victorious, and soon claimed back their own with interest.

This sketch of the fellow-workers of Shiváji in the task of national liberation would be incomplete without a brief notice of the holy men of peace, who about this time flourished in the country, and were the chief advisers of the civil and military commanders. The Chitnis's *Bakhar* makes mention of a number of these great teachers, chief among whom were the Moryádév of Chinchwad, Ranganáth Swámi of Nigadi, Vithalráo of Bédar Váman Joshi of Shingátá, Nimbáji Báwá of Dahitané, Bodhlé Báwá of Dhámangáon, Jayarám Swámi of Wadgáon, Késhav Swámi of Hyderábád, Paramánand Báwá of Poládpur, Achalpuri of Sangaméshvar and Mani Báwá of Padgáon. The most celebrated, however, of these spiritual teachers were Tukárám Báwá of Déhu and Rámdás Swámi of Cháfal. Rámdás became Shiváji's spiritual guide and his chief adviser even in secular matters. The influence of these religious teachers will be more fully noticed in a separate chapter. It will be sufficient here to state that by the influence of Rámdás and Tukárám the national sentiment was kept up at a higher level of spirituality and devotion to public affairs than it would otherwise have attained. In token of the work of liberation being carried on, not for personal aggrandisement but for higher purposes of service to God and man, the national standard received, at the suggestion of Rámdás, its favourite orange colour, which was and is the colour of the clothes worn by anchorites and devotees. The old forms of salutation were dispensed with as implying submission to the foreigner, and a new form was substituted, which only recited the name of Rámdás's favourite deity. Under the same influence the names of Shiváji's principal officers were changed from their Mahomedan designations to Sanskrit equivalents, and the forms of correspondence also were similarly improved. Shiváji, from a sense of gratitude to his spiritual teacher, made a gift of his kingdom, and Rámdás gave it back to him as a trust to be managed in the public interest. When Shiváji pressed him to accept some *Inám* lands for the service of his favourite diety, Rámdás significantly requested him to assign *Ináms* in territories which were still under foreign sway, thus significantly hinting that the work of liberation was not yet completed.

The short sketches given above of the leading men, who figured prominently about the time of the rise of the Maráthá power, will, it is hoped, convey a more accurate idea of the condition of the times than any chronicle of Shiváji's deeds. It was this back-ground behind Shivájis great central figure, which constituted the chief source of the wisdom and strength, which were put forth under his leadership. No account of Shiváji's life could be complete without a full realisation of the strength of the national awakening that had taken place at this time. The vitality of a nation is best presented not merely by its capacity for self-defence, but also by its power in each succeeding generation to raise up men fitted in every way to carry on the work with greater vigour and more assured success. Judged by this double test, Shiváji's contemporaries fully sustained their place as a generation of men at once wise and brave, who were worthily led by him in the work of national construction.

CHAPTER V.

THE TREE BLOSSOMS.

THE public career of Shiváji may be said to have commenced with the occupation of Toraná in 1646, when he was only nineteen years old, and his life of ceaseless activity was brought to a close prematurely in 1680. This period of thirty-four years naturally ranges itself into four divisions of unequal length, which must be studied apart, as the sphere of activity and the principles of conduct guiding that activity underwent a slow but decided change as Shiváji grew up in years and experience. Much confusion has resulted from ignoring the fact that this career was one of growth and development, and the rules of action which influenced Shiváji necessarily varied with the varying exigencies of his success in the earlier and later stages. In another respect also prejudice has been at work in applying to the wild times in which Shiváji's early years were passed the stricter standards of public morality, for which, even in Europe, modern civilization has only recently secured general recognition, instead of maxims of policy observed by contemporary native rulers in India and elsewhere. The Maráthá country proper had never been really conquered by the Moslem rulers of the Deccan. They had subjugated the plains, but the hilly portions to the west were only occasionally overrun. The forts were not garrisoned, nor kept in repair, and the *Killédárs,* who were generally men with local influence, were allowed to have very much their own way, pushing and jostling each other, and making wars and annexations, as though there were no central power to control their movements. The looseness of this system of anarchic rule was further aggravated by the fact that, with the break-up of the Nizámsháhi kingdom, its spoils had been shared by the Emperors of Delhi and the kings of Bijápur, and the Maráthá country was the constant scene of the border warfare of these two powers. The unhappy results of such a confusion of authority can be better imagined than described. In the first six years of his career, Shiváji busied himself with his unruly neighbours in command of the hill-forts and Mávals about Pooná, and he had no thought of defying the distant authority of the Moghul commanders at Aurangábád, or of the kings of Bijápur.

He had his own *Jahágir* about Pooná and Supá to protect, and he could only defend it with the least expense of money and men by seizing or repairing the neglected hill-forts which commanded it on all sides. Besides this immediate and practical concern of self-defence, Shiváji had, even in these early years of his life, a dominant idea of uniting together the scattered forces of the Maráthá chiefs in his neighbourhood, and thereby securing that general protection and toleration which past experience showed could not otherwise be ensured.

When this preliminary task was accomplished without bloodshed, and with the consent of all parties concerned, Shiváji found himself forced into a conflict with the power of the Bijápur kings, who first treacherously imprisoned his father, and sent emissaries to surprise and capture him, and afterwards tried to crush him by a series of invasions led by the most distinguished commanders in Bijápur service. This conflict with Bijápur formed the second period in the story of his life, and extended over ten years, at the end of which time, Shiváji succeeded in dictating his own terms and establishing his power more firmly than ever over a larger extent of territory than had come under his influence before the war commenced. The dominant idea was still the same,—of self-defence and of nationalizing the movement. The success he achieved in this second period brought him into contact with the Moghul invaders of the Deccan, and the story of this struggle with the Moghul power constitutes the main interest of his life during the third period, which commenced with 1662, and ended about 1672 with the victories which secured from the Moghul Emperor a full and formal recognition of the new Maráthá power. The fourth and the last period commences with the coronation in 1674 and ends with his death. His life and character are best studied in this the last period of what may be regarded as the full fruition of all his hopes and ambitions, and he should be judged by the principles of action and the system of Government to which he then gave effect. He never lost sight of the main aim of his policy. Self-protection from his neighbours developed into self-defence against the Moslem powers. His sole aim was the union of the scattered elements of Maráthá power, though the sphere of this unifying influence was gradually increased. He had no quarrel with the Bijápur kings, or with the Moghul

Emperors, so long as they confined themselves to their own proper spheres of action in the Karnátik and North India, and did not make aggressive warfare with a view to subjugate Western Maháráshtra. In fact, he extended his protection to the Golcondá kings who ruled in Télangan and also materially helped the kings of Bijápur to repel the attack made by the Moghuls upon that kingdom. As regards the Delhi Emperors, he was prepared to be their dependant vassal, if they would let his country alone. With this view he went all the way to Delhi to make his submission, and even after he had been treacherously put in confinement, he consented to an armistice, the principal condition of which was that the Emperor should recognize him as one of the chief nobles of the Empire. The idea of forming a confederacy of Hindu powers all over India, and subverting Musalman dominion, appeared never to have seriously been entertained by him It was a later growth, and was first realized by Bájiráo Ballál, when, in the conflict between him and Pant Pratinidhi, he advised Sháhu Maháràja not to waste his energies in lopping off the branches, but to use all available strength in shaking the tree by its roots at the centre of power near Delhi. Shiváji's idea seems to have been to form a central Hindu power in the Deccan, and in alliance with the Bijápur and Golcondá kings to push back the Moghul power to the north of the Tápti river. This is the clue to the whole situation. Self-defence and the formation of a national Hindu power in Western India, which, in alliance with the Mahomedan States of Golcondá and Bijápur, would repel aggression from the North, and enforce protection and toleration for his own countrymen,—these were the objects and limits of his ambition. With this clue in hand, we shall be better able to study the entanglements of the narrative of these four distinctive periods in the life and career of Shiváji.

The first period, as stated above, commences with the occupation of Toraná, whose *Killédár* gave it up. Ráigad was next fortified and made the principal seat of his residence. There was nothing very unusual in these proceedings, and the Bijápur *Darbár* was persuaded that these forts were seized in the general interest, and by way of protection to the family *Jahágir.* The displacement of Báji Mohité from the charge of Supá was an act of authority which could excite no comment, because he was a servant of the *Jahágir*. On the Eastern side, the Chákan fort commanded the way to Pooná, and Shiváji persuaded Firangoji Narasálé to make it over to him. The command of the Fort was left with Firangoji as before, and ever after he continued to be a most devoted adherent. The Mahomedan commander of the fort of Sinhagad to the west of Pooná was similarly persuaded to vacate his charge. The Mávals were thus brought under control, and the Mávlis, the hardy inhabitants of these parts, were enlisted in the army under their own natural leaders. All these accessions were made without any violence or blood-shed. The *Jahágir* included, besides Pooná and Supá, Bárámati and Indápur, and the Purandar fort commanded the old road from Pooná to Bárámati. The seizure of Purandar was desirable for these and other reasons. The old Bijápur commander was a Bráhman who was personally well disposed to Dádoji Kondadév, but was otherwise very lawless in his movements. His wife, having remonstrated against certain acts of his, was punished by being blown away from the mouth of a cannon. The death of this man led to disputes among his sons, and Shiváji was invited to settle those disputes. Shiváji made prisoners of the three brothers, and seized the Fort for himself. Mr. Grant Duff has characterised this conduct as treacherous. He, however, admits that the three brothers received grants of *Inám* lands, and rose to some distinction in Shiváji's service. The native chronicles show that there was a very strong party in the garrison who, apprehending trouble from the disputes of the three brothers, counselled Shiváji to take the place for himself. Two of the brothers also appeared to have been willing parties to the settlement effected. These considerations materially alter the character of the act, and show that Shiváji seized the fort for its strategic value, with the consent of the garrison.

It was in pursuance of Shiváji's general policy that all these forts were acquired without violence or blood-shed, and their acquisition marks the confidence that he had already inspired amongst his neighbours. The reduction of Rohidá in Hirdas Mával, and the forts along the range of the Sahyádri, northward up to Kalyán, and southward down to Pratápgad, including Lohagad and Ráiri, in a manner completed the conquests of this first period. The seizure of Kalyán roused the authorities at Bijápur, and they brought pressure to bear upon Shiváji through his father. Shaháji was recalled from his *Jahágir* in the Karnátik, and treacherously seized and thrown into prison. This danger to his father's life compelled Shiváji to abstain from further aggressions. He however, turned the tables by offering his services to the Moghul Emperor Shahájahán, and the protection of the Emperor was found effective enough to secure Shaháji's release from imprisonment. In the offer of service which Shiváji made to the Delhi Emperor on this occasion, we find mention made for the first time of the famous *Chouth* and *Sardêshmukhi* claims. Shahájahán is said to have promised considerations of these claims when Shiváji would visit Delhi to press them in person, an event which did not happen in Shahájahán's time. These events happened in 1652, with which year the first period may be said to have closed.

Shaháji's release in 1657 removed the restraint which had kept Shiváji comparatively inactive during the past few years. The Bijápur authorities also had patched up a peace with the Moghul commanders, and were thus free to turn their forces against Shiváji. The leading feature of this second period was the conflict with the Bijápur power. This conflict brought Shiváji in contact with the more powerful Maráthá *Jahágirdárs* in the Bijápur service. These were the Ghorpadés of Mudhol, the Morés of Jávli, the Sávants of Wádi, the Dalvis of South Konkan, the Mánés of Mhaswad, the Survés and the Shirkés of Shringárpur, the Nimbálkars of Faltan, and the Ghádgés of Málawdi. Shiváji's object during these years appears to have been to unite these chiefs, whose *Jahágirs* lay to the south of the Nirá and north of the Krishná, as he had united those who lived in his neighbourhood, under his leadership. His offers were, however, declined, and Chandraráo Moré, the most powerful of them, allowed his *Jahágirs* to be used as a protection to a party sent from Bijápur under a Bráhman *Sardár* Báji Shamaráj, with the intention of surprising Shiváji and assassinating him. The plot was discovered, and the Bijápur agents were in their turn surprised by Shiváji. This active hostility of Chandraráo Moré could not be safely put up with any longer, and Shiváji's agents, Rágho Ballál and Sambbáji Káwji, resolved on their own account to punish the Morés. The vengeance was swift and sure, but the deed was none the less to be censured, seeing that it was open and avowed treachery in return for what had only been a suspected connivance at treachery. The Maráthá chroniclers themselves attempt no defence of the murder of Chandraráo, and the only extenuating feature of the incident is that Shiváji's agents planned and carried it out on their own responsibility, though afterwards Shiváji accepted the results without much misgiving. The conquest of Jávli opened up the way to the subjugation of the country south of Pratápgad, down to the limits of Panhálá, as also the Southern Konkan, including the *Jahágirs* of the Sávants of Wádi, who made their submission. The Dalvis and the Survés who held *Jahágirs* in those parts were also reduced to submission. The Siddi's territory was also attacked, but without any decided result.

These successes brought matters to a crisis, and the Bijápur authorities resolved to make a supreme effort. They had found out that Shiváji was not amenable to his father's control, and that any pressure put upon him through his father only drove him to seek the support of the

Moghul Emperor. Their first army under Báji Shámaráj, who sought to surprise Shiváji unawares, had been defeated and Chandraráo Moré, on whom they relied, as also the Sávants and Dalvis, had found themselves unable to hold their place against Shiváji's generals. This time therefore they resolved to send an overwhelming force under their ablest Pathán general Afzulkhán. Afzulkhán had taken part in the Karnátik wars, and with or without reason had been suspected as having helped Shaháji's enemies there and brought about the untimely death of Shiváji's elder brother. Afzulkhán had ostentatiously undertaken in open *Darbár* at Bijápur to capture the mountain rat, as he called Shiváji, dead or alive. On his way from Bijápur to Wái, Afzulkhán desecrated the great temples at Tuljápur and Pandharpur, and broke the idols. His march therefore had all the appearance of a religious war, and naturally excited the worst passions on both sides. There can be no doubt that the issues which depended upon the result of this contest were of the gravest possible character. It was a struggle of life or death to the victor or the vanquished. Shiváji and his councillors perceived the gravity of the situation. They prepared themselves to repel the invasion, but before Shiváji adopted his final plans, he invoked the guidance of his goddess Bhawáni. He asked his *Chitnis* to note down in writing the words which the goddess might put into his own mouth, while he was under the influence of divine possession. The words were noted down as they were uttered in unconscious excitement.

Encouraged by the promise of protection thus assured, and by the blessing of his mother, and the devotion of his army, Shiváji resolved to meet his great antagonist on a spot carefully chosen by himself. While all this care and caution were being bestowed on the part of Shiváji, Afzulkhán, proud in the possession of the large army that he was leading, and certain that Shiváji would not stand up against him in the field, was intent upon one subject only, namely, to bring out Shiváji from the shelter of his forts, and, if possible, to capture him and take him in triumph to Bijápur, and thus avoid all the perils of a long campaign. While Shiváji's army occupied the valleys of the Krishná and Koyaná, and the thick jungles concealed them from the enemies' view, Afzulkhán's army spread from Wái to Mahábaleshwar, exposed to flank attacks on both sides. Apparently each was anxious to surprise and capture the other's person, for both knew that in eastern warfare the fall of the General leading the army too often determined or greatly influenced the result of the fight. Afzulkhán was approached by Shiváji's emissaries who represented to him that Shiváji was ready to make his submission, and thereupon Afzulkhán sent his own Bráhman Pandit to obtain correct information. This man was gained over by an appeal to his religious and patriotic sentiments. It was then arranged that both should meet one another for personal explanations unattended by their forces. What happened at the interview has been variously described. The Mahomedan historians, whom Grant Duff follows, charge Shiváji with treachery in the first attack he made with the fatal *Wágha-nakha* (tiger-claws) and the Bhawáni sword; while the Maráthá chroniclers, both Sabhásada and Chitnis, state that the stalwart Khán first seized Shiváji's neck by the left hand and, drawing him towards himself, caught him under his left arm, and it was not till the Khán's treachery was thus manifested that Shiváji dealt the fatal blow. In those times the practice of treachery on such occasions was a very common occurrence, and it may be presumed that both Afzulkhán and Shiváji were prepared for such a risk. Shiváji had on his side strong motives; he had his brother's death and the desecration of the Tuljápur and Pandharpur temples to avenge. He knew he was then unequal to face the enemy in the open field. The success of all that he had achieved and planned during the past twelve years depended on the result. He had therefore stronger motives to effect his purpose by stratagem than his enemy. The personal character of the two men must also be considered. The one was apparently vain and reckless, while the other was supremely self-possessed and never beside his guard. The arrangements that Shiváji had made for a surprise of the Mahomedan army as soon as Afzulkhán was disposed of, and the perfect confusion which followed the attack made by the Maráthás, also showed that while Shiváji was prepared to follow up the result of the personal interview, Afzulkhán's people were wholly unprepared to resist such an attack. These considerations certainly lend support to the view to which Mr. Grant Duff has given the weight of his authority. The fact may well be that where both parties are mutually suspicious of each other, each may have misjudged the most innocent motions of the other, and he who had taken the least precautions naturally suffered for his folly. The will to do mischief might have been equally operative on both sides, though one was not prepared to take full advantage of the situation as it developed itself to the same extent as the other was. The fall of Afzulkhán led to the conquest of the countries southward to Panhálá and along the banks of the Krishná. A second army sent by the Bijápur Government was defeated, and Shiváji followed up the rout by pushing his army to the very gates of Bijápur, while his Generals captured Rájápur and Dábhol. A third army was sent from Bijápur which besieged Panhálá, while Shiváji and his forces were resting in that fort. By the use of stratagem Shiváji made his escape to Ránganá, while the Bijápur army in pursuit was kept at bay in a narrow defile, which might be described as the Thermopylæ of Maráthá history guarded by Báji Prabhu and one thousand Mávlis, who kept up the fight for more than nine hours till they had lost three quarters of the men, and the gallant Báji Prabhu, their commander, died at his post, but not till he had heard the signal gun of Shiváji's safe arrival at Ránganá. A fourth expedition was led by the Bijápur king in person in 1661-1662, but no important advantage was gained, and the war lingered on for a year and more. It was about this time that Shiváji first organized his fleet, and made himself master of all the Konkan sea-forts, except that of Janjirá. In 1662 the Bijápur Government found its resources so thoroughly exhausted by the long struggle that had been waged that the good offices of Sháháji were again utilized by them, and a peace was concluded, by which Shiváji was left master of all the territories he had brought under his influence. At the end of the first period Shiváji's possessions extended from Chákan to the river Nirá and included his own *jahágir*, and the forts in the Sahyádri range from Purandar to Kalyán. At the end of the second period, Shiváji's possessions included the whole of the Konkan from Kalyán to Goá, and the Ghátmáthá districts parallel to this coast line, from the river Bhimá to the river Wárná, about one hundred and sixty miles north to south and one hundred miles to the east of the Ghát range. The Bijápur kings broke the conditions of this treaty at a later stage in the third period of Shiváji's struggles with the Delhi Emperors. But

Pratápráo Gujar, Shivájí's Commander-in-Chief, repelled that attack on the first occasion, but allowed the enemy to escape back to their country. Shiváji found fault with his General for his leniency in pursuit, and Pratápráo was so touched by his master's rebuke that, when next the Bijápur Generals again invaded Shiváji's possessions, Pratápráo again defeated them with great slaughter, and hotly pursued them this time at the sacrifice of his own precious life. When Bijápur later on was besieged by the Moghuls, the king of Bijápur made an earnest appeal for help to Shiváji, and he on his part, forgetting the injuries that had been done to him, attacked the invading Moghuls from behind, and on the flanks, and by carrying the war into the Moghul territory, forced them to raise the siege. This generous help saved Bijápur this time, and gave it a new lease of life for twenty years more. These events have their proper place in the third period, but are mentioned here mainly for the sake of bringing together in one view the history of Shiváji's relations with Bijápur.

CHAPTER VI.

THE TREE BEARS FRUIT.

THE third period commences with 1662. Down to that year, Shiváji had studiously refrained from coming into conflict with the Moghul armies occupying the Deccan, and excepting a single plundering expedition to Junnar in 1657, there had been no act of overt hostility on either side. In fact in Shahájahán's time, Shiváji had made offers of submission to that Emperor, not only with a view to bring pressure on the Bijápur kings for the release of his father, but also with a view to secure a recognition for certain claims in his own interest, which Shahájahán promised to consider favourably when Shiváji pressed them in person as a suitor in his court. When Aurangzéb abandoned the siege of Bijápur, and proceeded hastily to fight with his brothers for the Delhi throne, he left instructions behind, by which Shiváji's claims to the Konkan were recognized, and it was suggested that he should serve the Emperor with a picked body of horse, and maintain tranquility in the imperial district south of the

Narmadá. When Aurangzéb had overcome the opposition of his brothers, and become the undisputed master of the Imperial throne, the understanding which had been established between him and Shiváji was not respected, and in 1661 a Moghul army seized Kalyán, which was the most northerly post occupied by Shiváji. Shiváji was unable to resent this attack till the peace with Bijápur was concluded in 1662, when Shiváji's General, Nétáji Pálkar, led the first expedition to Aurangábád, and the Péshwá Moropant seized forts to the north of Junnar, which was then the most advanced Moghul outpost in Maráthá country proper. The war thus commenced in right earnest on both sides. Sháhistékhán, the Moghul commander, seized Pooná and Chákan, and made the former place his head-quarters. Sháhistékhán was surprised by a night attack in his own palace at Pooná, and the Moghul cavalry who went in pursuit of Shiváji, as he retreated from Pooná to Sinhagad, was defeated by Nétáji Pálkar. These events happened in 1663, and in 1664 Shiváji led his famous first expedition through an unknown country without any opposition against Surat, which was then the emporium of Indian commerce with foreign countries. The Maráthá navy also captured pilgrim ships bound from Surat to Meccá. Another portion of the fleet plundered a rich port to the south of Goá in 1665, and as a result of this expedition, Shiváji established his authority in north Kanará. Sháhistékhán never rallied from the defeat he had sustained in the night surprise at Pooná, and had to be recalled, and a second army under the famous Rájá Jayasingh and Dilérkhán was sent in 1665 to accomplish the task of reducing Shiváji's power. The Moghul army entered the Maráthá country unopposed, and finally laid siege to Purandar. The fort was defended by a Prabhu commander, named Murár Báji Déshpándé, of Mahád. He maintained the unequal contest till he was killed. For reasons not sufficiently explained either in the native chronicles or by Mr. Grant Duff, Shiváji was at this time persuaded that the most politic course for him was to make his submission to Rájá Jayasingh, who was then the premier Hindu nobleman at the Delhi court, and to effect by peaceful means the aims he had in view. This resolution was not suddenly adopted in a moment of despondency. The native chronicle states that Shiváji appealed for guidance to divine help, and the goddess Bhawáni counselled him to make his submission at the time, as Jayasingh was also a favourite with the gods, and success against him could not be secured by continuing the war. Seeing that Shiváji had so easily defeated Afzulkhán and Sháhistékhán, and that later on when Aurangzéb with his whole army occupied the Deccan, the Maráthá Generals were able to carry on the war against him without any recognized leader, and with no single fort in their occupation, it cannot be for a moment supposed that Shiváji was unable to continue his contest with Jayasingh on equal terms. Throughout his career of thirty four years, Shiváji did not on a single occasion suffer defeat where he led his armies in person, and even when his affairs were at the worst, he seemed to gather new courage and resource from the inspiration of the dangers about him. We may therefore take it for granted that when he deliberately offered to submit to Jayasingh and make over most of his forts and territories, there must have been some deep-laid scheme of policy which justified to him and his councillors the course he pursued. Shiváji might well have thought that his temporary submission and visit to Delhi would introduce him to a larger sphere of action, or at least would enable him to make the acquaintance of the great Rajput nobles of the empire. Jayasingh's friendship, cemented by such an act of self-sacrifice, might prove helpful in the furtherance of his larger designs. Shiváji had been always urging his claims to *chouth* and *sardéshmukhi*, and though these claims had not been recognized either by Aurangzéb or Shahájahán, hopes had been held out which encouraged him to think that by temporary submission he might secure a legitimate basis for the assertion of these claims. These, and considerations like these, might have had more weight allowed to them than the course of future events proved to be reasonable, but it is certain that on this occasion, Shiváji was resolved to make his peace with the Emperor at any price. A truce was accordingly arranged. Twenty forts were made over into the Moghul charge, while twelve were retained in the hands of Shiváji's commanders. A Council of Regency was formed of his three most trusted advisers with Jijábái at its head, and Shiváji entered the Moghul service, and marched, with Jayasingh as his companion, against Bijápur. Later on, when assurances of personal safety had been obtained, Shiváji went with his son and a considerable body of horse and Mávlis to Delhi, where he was received by the Emperor rather coldly, and he soon found out that he had made the only great mistake in his life. The stratagem by which he escaped is too well known to need detailed repetition here. But it showed Shivája at his best in the resourcefulness with which he could surmount obstacles, and it also signally tried the devotion of his followers. He reached his country ten months after he had left it, and found everything just in the condition in which he had left it. This visit to Delhi represented the first great crisis in Maráthá history. The Moghul armies occupied the plains and the forts; Shivája and his son were prisoners in Delhi; and yet there was not a single person who proved traitor to his country or joined the enemy. The government was carried on as if nothing had happened. Everybody remained firm at his post, and when the news arrived that he had escaped from Delhi and returned home, it spread like wildfire, and the war was recommenced with greater ardour and vigor than before. Fort after fort was besieged and reconquered. Moropant Péshwá had in fact, even before Shivája reached his native land, taken advantage of the recall of Jayasingh to seize the forts north of Pooná and a greater portion of the province of Kalyán. The Emperor sent a third army under his son with Jaswantsingh, the Ráná of Jodhpur, in place of Rájá Jayasingh as commander. The emperor's son was appointed Viceroy of the Deccan, and his first act as Viceroy was to conclude an arrangement with Shiváji with the consent of his father. Under this arrangement, Aurangzéb granted the title of Rájá to Shiváji, and gave a *mansab* to Shiváji's son of five thousand horse, and a *jahágir* to Shiváji himself in the Bérárs in lieu of his claims over Junnar and Ahmednagar. The old *jahágir* districts of Pooná, Chákan, and Supá were also restored back to him, with the exception of Sinhagad and Purandar. By this arrangement, Shiváji became a noble of the Empire, and engaged to serve the Emperor with a considerable body of horse, who were stationed near Aurangábád under the charge of Pratápráo Gujar. This arrangement lasted for two years, till the war with Bijápur carried on by the Moghul Emperors was concluded in 1669.

Shiváji was not a party to the treaty then made between the Bijápur kings and the Moghul commanders, but in consideration of the good understanding then prevalent between the Viceroy of the Deccan and Shiváji, his claims to *chouth* and *sardéshmuhki*, which had been several times urged by him before, were in 1669 for the first time recognized by the kings of Golcondá and Bijápur, who agreed to pay respectively five and three lakhs of rupees to Shiváji in lieu of those claims. This recognition must have been the result of an understanding arrived at between the parties, including the Moghul commanders in the Deccan. Shiváji's position in 1669 was thus considerably strengthened. He got back his *jahágirs* and most of the hill-forts. He secured a *mansab* and a *jahágir* from the emperor, and he further secured the recognition of his claims to levy *chouth* and *sardéshmukhi* from the Mahomedan kingdoms in the Deccan. With these advantages, Shiváji was enabled to carry on with greater chances of success the war when it was forced upon him by Aurangzéb's violation of the understanding that had been established in 1667. Aurangzéb ordered his son, the Deccan Viceroy, to apprehend Shiváji by force or stratagem under penalty of his severe displeasure. Pratápráo Gujar, who was stationed at Aurangábád with his contingent of Maráthá horse, obtained news of this intended treachery, and managed to escape. Shiváji thus found himself again face to face with the whole power of the Emperor of Delhi. The necessity of self-defence suggested the recapture of Sinhagad which had for the last five years been garrisoned by Rajputs in the imperial service. Tánáji Málusaré led the attack, and scaled the walls, with his three-hundred Mávlis, at dead of night, and effected the entrance, but only to meet death at the hands of the garrison. His brother Suryáji completed the work with heroism worthy of the great sacrifice his brother Tánáji had offered in his own person for the cause of his country. Purandar, Máhuli, Karnálá, Lohagad, and Junnar were carried by storm. Janjirá was attacked, but the Siddis were able by their superior strength on the sea to hold their forts. Surat was plundered a second time. It was on his return from Surat that Shiváji was overtaken by the Moghul commanders in pursuit of him, and though greatly outnumbered, the Maráthá horse succeeded not only in sending their plunder safe to Ráigad, but in routing the pursuers with heavy loss. Pratápráo Gujar entered Khándésh, levying contributions throughout the District and penetrated further east into the Bérárs. This was the first occasion when *sardéshmukhi* and *chouth* were levied from provinces subject to the Delhi Emperors. Moropant Péshwá also in 1671 took several forts, including Salher in Báglan. Next year this fort was besieged by Moghul commanders with a great army. The Maráthás not only stood the siege bravely, but Moropant Péshwá and Pratápráo succeeded in defeating the Moghul army in a pitched battle. In 1673, Panhálá was retaken, and Hubli was plundered by one of Shiváji's generals, Annáji Datto. A naval expendition was sent to Kárwár, and the whole of the coast districts in that part of the country were reconquered, and the Rájá of Bédnore was made a tributary like the king of Golcondá. An army sent from Bijápur was defeated with heavy loss by Pratápráo Gujar, and on a renewal of the attack in 1674, Hansáji Mohité again defeated the Bijápur forces, and pursued them to the gates of Bijápur. Thus in four years from the renewal of hostilities, Shiváji succeeded in regaining all his old possessions and in greatly extending his conquests in all directions, both by sea and land. In the North he penetrated as far as Surat, in the South as far as Hubli and Bédnore, in the East as far as Bérárs, Bijápur and Golcondá. *Chouth* and *sardéshmuki* were levied from the Moghul *Subhás* south of the

Tápti, and the chiefs of Golcondá and Bédnore were made tributaries. In the words of the native chroniclers, Shiváji had vindicated his claims to be the Pádsháhá of the Hindus, after having defeated the forces of the three Musalman Pádsháhás, and forced them to yield submission to his claims. This naturally suggested to Shiváji and his council the idea of a formal coronation ceremony which would fitly celebrate the greatness of the work accomplished by nearly thirty years' incessant efforts, and in the then disordered condition of Southern India furnish a rallying centre to all the Deccan chiefs to resist with a united effort the apprehended danger of Aurangzéb's great invasion.

We thus enter upon the fourth and the last period of Shiváji's career. The coronation ceremony ushered it in with proper pomp and festivities. The fact of the establishment of a powerful Hindu kingdom had to be proclaimed with due solemnity and every hill-fort along the Sahyádri range, as also on the sea coast proclaimed the event by cannon salvoes all over the country. During the remaining portion of Shiváji's life he was comparatively left to himself by the Moghul commanders, who directed their efforts chiefly to the conquest of Bijápur and Golcondá. An attack made by the Moghul commander on Golcondá was frustrated by the timely arrival of Hambirráo Mohité, and the king of Golcondá was safe for a time under the protection of Shiváji, and actually helped him with his own forces in the expedition against the Karnátik, which Shiváji led in person, and in the course of which he penetrated as far south as Tanjore, and seized Véllore, fortified Gingi, and established military posts all along the line of the road through Mysore. Bijápur was very hard-pressed by the Moghul commanders who laid siege to the city. The Adilsháhi kings and councillors had no resource left but to turn to Shiváji for help, and notwithstanding the memories of past wrongs, Shiváji lent the help of his army, which devastated the Moghul country from Surat to Barhánpur, and attacked the flanks and rear of the invading army, and thus forced the Moghul commanders to raise the siege, and return to Aurangábád. These were the only important military events of this period, which was chiefly distinguished for the reforms in civil administration, carried out and completed by Shiváji during the comparative leisure he found about this time.

We shall briefly notice these reforms in the next chapter. It will suffice here to state that, while at the end of the first period Shiváji's influence was confined to the strip of country lying between Chákan and the Nirá river, at the time of his death he was the most powerful native ruler south of the river Tápti, and his paramount influence was acknowledged both by Hindu and Mahomedan sovereigns from the Tápti to the Kávéri.

CHAPTER VII.

SHIVAJI AS A CIVIL RULER.

THE history of Shiváji's military exploits only presents to our view one side of the working of his master mind, and we are too apt to forget that he had other and stronger claims upon our attention as a civil ruler. Like the first Napoleon, Shiváji in his time was a great organiser, and a builder of civil institutions, which conduced largely to the success of the movement initiated by him, and which alone enabled the country to pass unscathed through the dangers which overwhelmed it shortly after his death, and helped it to assert its claim to national independence, after a twenty years' struggle with the whole power of the Moghul Empire. These civil institutions deserve special study because they display an originality and breadth of conception which he could not have derived from the systems of government then prevalent under Mahomedan or Hindu rule; and what is still more noteworthy is that when after the war of independence, the country was reorganized, his own successors returned to the traditions of the past, and departed from the lines laid down by the founder of the Maráthá power, and in so departing from the model he had set up, they sowed the seeds of that disunion and separation which it was his constant solicitude to avoid in all that he attempted and achieved. As has been stated before, Shiváji did not aspire to found an universal empire under his own direct rule throughout India. He strove to secure the freedom of his own people, and unite them into one nation, powerful for self-defence, and for self-assertion also; but the extinction of all other powers was not contemplated by him. He had friendly relations with the Chiefs of Golcondá and Bédnore, and even Bijápur, and did not interfere with their respective spheres of influence, in the Télangan, Mysore and Karnátik countries, and he allowed his brother Vénkoji to retain his father's *jahágir*, all to himself, in the Dravid country. He contented himself with levying only *chouth* and *sardéshmukhi* from the Moghul possessions. He made a clear distinction between *Swarájya* (territory directly governed by him), and *Moglái* (that governed by foreign kings outside his *Swarájya*). The civil institutions founded by him were intended chiefly for the Maráthá country proper, though they were also introduced partially in the line of military forts, maintained by him to the extreme south of the Peninsula. The civil territory, held under his direct sway, was divided into a number of *Pránts* (Districts). Besides his ancestral *jahágir* about Pooná, there was (1) Pránt Mával—corresponding with Mával, Sáswad, Junnar, and Khéd Tálukás of the present day, and guarded by eighteen great hill-forts; (2) the Pránts of Wái, Sátárá, and Karád—corresponding with the Western portions of the present Sátárá district, guarded by fifteen forts; (3) Pránt Panhálá—corresponding with the western parts of Kolhápur, with thirteen hill-forts; (4) Pránt South Konkan—corresponding with Ratnágiri, with fifty-eight hill-forts and sea fortresses; (5) Pránt Tháná—corresponding with North Konkan District, with twelve forts; (6-7) Pránts Trimbak and Báglan—corresponding with the western parts of Násik, with sixty-two hill-forts. The territories occupied by the military garrisons were, (8) Pránt Wanagad—corresponding with the southern parts of Dhárwár district, with twenty-two forts; (9, 10, 11) Prants Bédnore, Kolhar, and Shrirangpatan—corresponding with the modern Mysore, with eighteen forts; (12) Pránt Karnátik, being the ceded districts in the Madrás Presidency south of the Krishná, with eighteen forts; (13) Piánt Véllore—modern Arcot districts, with twenty-five forts; and (14) Piánt Tanjore, with six forts. The whole of the Sahyádri range was studded with forts, and the territories to the west as far as the sea, and to the east of these forts, varied in breadth from fifty to one hundred miles at the most.

The chronicles make mention of some two hundred and eighty forts in Shiváji's occupation. In one sense it might be said that the hill-forts, with the territory commanded by it, was the unit of Shiváji's civil government. He spared no money in building new, and repairing old forts, and his arrangements about the garrisoning and provisioning of these forts were of the most elaborate kind. The military exploits which made these forts so famous, as points of resistance against attack, or centres of aggression, formed the chief interest of these early Maráthá wars. The Empire was knit together by the chain of these hill-forts, and they were its saviours in days of adversity. In the Sátárá district, Sátárá itself stood a siege for many months against Aurangzéb's whole power, and though it was stormed at last, it was the first fort which was taken back from the Moghuls under Rájárám's leadership by the ancestors of the present chief of Aundh. Toraná and Ráigad are associated with the first conquests of Shiváji, Shivanéri was his birthplace, Purandar was made memorable by Báji Prabhu's defence, and Rohidá and Sinhagad will always be associated with the memory of the brave Tánáji Málusaré; Panhálá stood the famous siege by Siddi Johár, while Ránganá was famous for another defence by Báji Prabhu of the defile which led to it at the sacrifice of his life. The Málwan fort and Kolábá were the places where the Maráthá navy was fitted out for its expeditions by sea. Pratápgad was made famous as the place of Afzulkhán's tragedy, while Máhuli and Sáléri were scenes of great battles in which the Maráthá Mávlis defeated the Moghul commanders. The extreme limits on the east side of these hill-forts of Shiváji's possessions were marked by the fortresses of Kalyán, Bhinwadi, Wái, Karád, Supá, Khatáv, Bárámati, Chákan, Shirawal, Miraj, Tásgaon, and Kolhápur. The important part played by these forts justified the care Shiváji bestowed on them. Each fort was under a Maráthá *Haváldár*, who had under him other assistants, in charge of each circular wall of defence, from the same class, and he was assisted by a Bráhman *Subhédár*, or *Sabnis*, chosen from the three great divisions of Bráhmans, and a *Kárkhánnis* who was a Prabhu. The *Haváldár*, with his assistants, had the military charge of the garrison. The Bráhman *Subhédár* had the civil and revenue charge, and this charge included the villages within the command of the fort, while the Prabhu officer was in charge of the grain and fodder and military stores and of the repairs. The three classes were thus joined together in a division of work, which ensured fidelity, and prevented jealousy. The hill-sides were carefully protected by strict conservancy, and the charge of the forests below the forts was entrusted to the *Rámoshis* and other lower classes of the population. Minute directions were given as to the way in which watch and ward duties were to be performed by day and night. The garrison varied in numbers according to the size and importance of the forts. There was a *Náik* for every nine Sepoys, and the arms were guns, short swords, javelins, spears and *pattás*—long thin swords. Each man received in cash and kind fixed amounts as wages for service according to his rank.

Coming down from the hill-forts to the plains, the country was divided into *Mahâls* and *Prânts*, very much on the plan now in force in our *Tâlukâ* system. The average revenue of a *Mahâl* ranged from three-fourths of a lakh to a lakh and a quarter, and two or three *mahâls* made a *Subhâ* or a district. The average pay of a *Subhêdâr* was four hundred *Hons* per year *i.e.*, about Rs. 100 per month. Shiváji did not continue the old Moghul system of leaving the revenue management solely in the hands of the village *Pâtils* or *Kulkarnis* or of *Déshmukhs* and *Déshpândés* of the district. These village and district authorities received their dues as before, but the work of management was taken out of their hands, and carried on directly by the *Subhêdârs* or *Mahâlkaris* for the *Subhâ* or the *Mahâl*, while every group of two or three villages was managed by a *Kamâvisdâr* (Kárkun), who made the direct collection of the revenue. The plan of farming out land revenue, either of villages or *mahâls* found no support under Shiváji's system.

The gradations of officers and men in the garrisons of the hill-forts were only copied from the regulations which were enforced by Shiváji both in his infantry and in his cavalry. In each infantry corps there was a *Náik* for every ten soldiers, one *Havál-dár* had charge of five such parties, two *Haválás* made one *Jumálédár*, ten *Jumálás* made a full corps of one thousand men under a *Hazári*, and seven *Hazáris* made up a *Sarnobat's* charge for the Mávli infantry. In the cavalry, there were two divisions, *Bárgirs* and *Silédárs*, and twenty-five *Bárgirs* or *Silédárs* had a *Havildár* over them, five *Haválás* made one *Jumálá*, ten *Jumálás* made a *Hazári's* charge, and five *Hazári* charges made one *Panch Hazári*. The *Panch Hazári* was under the *Sarnobat* of the cavalry. Every batch of twenty-five horses had one water-carrier and farrier. Under each of the higher Maráthá officers, both in the infantry and cavalry, there was a Bráhman *Sabnis* and a Prabhu *Kárkhánnis* or a Bráhman *Muzumdár* and Prabhu *Jáminis*. The *Bárgir's* horses were during the monsoons cantoned in camps, where every provision was made for grass and grain supplies, and barracks were built for the men to live under shelter. All the officers and men received fixed pay, which in the case of the *Págá Hazári*, was one-thousand *Hons*, and *Págá Panch Hazári*, two-thousand *Hons*. In the case of the infantry, the pay was five-hundred *Hons* for the *Hazári*, and for the lower officers and men the pay varied from Rs. 9 to 3 for the infantry, and Rs. 20 to 6 in the cavalry, according to the higher or lower rank of the soldier or trooper. During eight months in the year the armies were expected to maintain themselves by *mulukhagiri*, *i.e.*, by levying *chouth* and *sardéshmukhi* from the Moghul Districts. When engaged on such service, the men were strictly prohibited from taking their women and children with them. When a city was plundered, the loot had to be accounted for by each soldier and trooper. No soldier or trooper was enlisted without taking a security bond from his fellows to insure good conduct. The military commanders were paid in advance, as they had to account for the *chouth* and *sardéshmukhi* collected by them. No assignments of revenue or land were allowed for the service of the army in Shiváji's time. Notwithstanding these strict restraints there was no difficulty found about the enlistment of recruits in the army, and no service was more popular than that which led the Mávlis of the Ghátmáthá and the Hétkaris of the Konkan, and the *Silédárs* and *Bárgirs* of Maháráshtra proper, to flock in numbers to the national standard on each *Dasará* day, when a call was made for their services.

This system of cash payment and direct revenue management was introduced and extended by Shiváji throughout his dominions. Native chroniclers notice this departure from old traditions in these two points more prominently because Shiváji appears to have laid great stress on it. It was his conviction that much of the disorder in old times was due to the entrusting of revenue duties to *Zamindárs* of Districts and villages. They collected more from the *rayats*, and paid less into the treasury than was strictly due, and used their opportunities to create disturbances and to resist the commands of the central power. Shiváji engaged the services of paid men—*Kamávisdárs*, *Mahálkaris*, and *Subhédárs*,—for the duties till then performed by *Zamindárs*. It was the *Kamávisdár's* duty to levy the grain and cash payments while the crops were standing. The fields were carefully measured out, and entered in books in the name of the holders thereof, and annual *kabuláyats* were taken from them for the payments due. In the case of grain payments, the Government assessment never exceeded two-fifths of the actual yield. The remaining three-fifths were left to the cultivator as his share of the crops. In times of distress, or in case of accident, *tagâi* advances were made liberally, and their recovery provided for by instalments spread over four or five years. The *Subhédârs* performed both revenue and criminal duties. The work of Civil Courts was not then of much importance, and when disputes arose, parties were referred by the *Subhêdâr* to the *Panch* of the villages, or to those of other villages in important cases, and enforced their decisions.

The Civil organization of the District was, of course, subordinate to the authorities at head-quarters, two of whom—the *Pant Amâtya* and the *Pant Sachiv*, had respectively the charge of what in our time would be called the office of Finance Minister and the General Accountant and Auditor. The district accounts had to be sent to these officers, and were there collated together, and irregularities detected and punished. These officers had power to depute men on their establishments to supervise the working of the district officers. The *Pant Amâtya* and the *Sachiv* were, next to the *Péshwâ*, the highest civil officers, and they had, besides these revenue duties, military commands. They were both important members of the Board of Administration, called the *Ashta Pradhán* or Cabinet of eight heads of departments. The *Péshwá* was Prime Minister, next to the king, and was at the head of both the civil and military administration, and sat first on the right hand below the throne. The *Sénápati* was in charge of the military administration, and sat first on the left side. *Amátya* and *Sachiv* sat next to the *Péshwá,* while the *Mantri* sat next below the *Sachiv,* and was in charge of the king's private affairs. The *Sumant* was Foreign Secretary, and sat below the *Sénápáti* on the left. Next came *Panditráo,* who had charge of the ecclesiastical department, and below him on the left side sat the Chief Justice. It will be seen from these details that the *Ashta Pradhán* system has its counterpart in the present constitution of the Government of India. The Governor-General and Viceroy occupies the place of the *Péshwá*; next comes the Commander-in-Chief of the army. The Finance and Foreign Ministers come next. In the Government of India, the Executive Council makes no room for the head of the ecclesiastical department, or for the Chief Justice on one side and the Private Secretary on the other, and in their place sit the Member in Charge of the Home Department, the Legal Member, and the Public Works Minister. These variations are due to the difference of circumstances, but the conception which lies at the bottom of both systems is the same, of having a council of the highest officers of the State, sitting together to assist the king in the proper discharge of his duties. If this system could have been loyally worked out by the successors of Shiváji, as it was originally conceived and worked by Shiváji himself, many of the dangers which ultimately destroyed the Maráthá confederacy, even before it came in conflict with the superior discipline and resources of the British power, might have been avoided. The seeds of dissolution lay in the fact that the necessities of the times required all the eight *Pradháns* or Ministers, except *Panditráo* and *Nyáyádhish*, to be military commanders, and these military commands necessarily placed power in the hands of the most successful leaders of the army. Shiváji himself carefully guarded against this danger by providing that none of these offices should be hereditary. In his own time he had four different Commanders-in-Chief, viz., Mánkoji Dahátondé, Nétáji Pálkar, Pratápráo Gujar, and Hambirráo

Mohité. He deprived the first *Péshwá* of his office, and gave it to Moropant Pinglé. The *Pant Amátya's* office similarly changed hands, and in fact the other offices were not allowed to be hereditary in particular families. This caution was, to some extent, observed in the early years of Sháhu's reign, but towards its end the talents and power of the first three *Péshwás,* Báláji Vishvanáth, the first Bájiráo, and Báláji Bájiráo, made the *Péshwáship* hereditary in their family, whilst the representatives of the other ministers were mostly incapable men, and their importance dwindled in consequence, and the equal distribution and balance of power was destroyed. Throughout the *Péshwás'* rule, the *Ashta Pradháns,* or the eight hereditary ministers of State, had no functions, or only nominal functions to discharge, and instead of being the organised government, which Shiváji designed it to be, we find an unorganised power of the old Asiatic type, depending solely for its vitality upon the capacity of the chief centre of power. Shiváji's system cannot be blamed for such a consequence. It was the departure from his system that was responsible for the failure of his plans.

In another respect also, Shiváji was far in advance of his times. He set himself steadily against any assignments of land as *jahágir* to his successful civil or military commanders. Every one from the *Péshwá* and *sénápati* down to the lowest sepoy or *kárkun* was, under Shiváji's arrangements, directed to draw his salary in kind or money from the public treasury and granaries. The salaries were fixed and paid regularly at stated periods. The assignment system was condemned because it was liable to be abused under the best circumstances, and with the best motives. The *Jahágirdár* naturally tends to become a territorial or feudal landlord, and when his influence is strengthened by hereditary connections, he cannot be removed except by force. The centrifugal tendencies towards separation and disunion are always naturally very strong in India, and the system of assigning *jahágirs*, and permitting the *Jahágirdár* to maintain a force of his own out of the revenue of the land assigned to him, aggravates this tendency to a degree which makes well-ordered rule almost impossible. Shiváji would not even allow *Zamindárs* of the District to build forts for their protection, but required them to live in houses unprotected like those of the *rayats*. None of the great men, who distinguished themselves in Shiváji's time, were able to hand over to their descendants large landed estates. Neither Moropant Pinglé nor Ábáji Sondév, nor Rágho Ballál or Datto Annáji or Niráji Ráoji, among the Bráhmans, nor the Málusarés or Kanks, or Pratápráo Gujar, Nétáji Pálkar, Hambirráo Mohité or the Maráthá *Sardárs*, were able to found ancient families such as those which Sháhu's ministers in the early part of the eighteenth century succeeded in doing.

The only assignments of land which Shiváji sanctioned in his time were intended for the endowment of temples and charities. These were public trusts, and the holders thereof had no military duties to discharge and could not, in the ordinary course of things, become dangerous to the State. Among the charities, the *Dakshiná* system of encouraging learning found strong support with Shiváji. It was an old edition of our modern system of payment by results. Bráhmans received *Dakshiná* according to scale which was carefully graduated so as to provide both for the extent and quality of learning acquired. There were no public schools in those days, but private teachers taught pupils in their own homes, and both teacher and pupil were placed above want by means of a judicious distribution of annual rewards. Sanskrit learning was at its lowest ebb in these parts when Shiváji rose to power, but by the methods of encouragement adopted by him, the Deccan soon became known for the proficiency of her scholars who proceeded to Benares for purposes of study, and returned back to their country laden with honours, and rewarded by their sovereign. The *Dakshiná* system of encouraging learning was, after Sambháji's capture by the Moguls, kept up by the Dábhádés of Talégaon, and when the Dábhádés lost their importance, the *Péshwás* took up the trust, and greatly enlarged its scope, and it flourished down to the times of the British conquest, when the amount disbursed each year is said to have exceeded five lakhs.

It will be seen from the details given above that Shiváji's system of Civil Government was distinguished from those which preceded it or succeeded it in several important respects :—

Firstly.—In the great importance he attached to the hill-forts, which were virtually the starting unit of his system of Government.

Secondly—In his discouragement of the hereditary system of transmitting high offices in one and the same family.

Thirdly—In his refusal to grant *jahágir* assignments of land for the support of Civil or Military Officers.

Fourthly—In the establishment of a direct system of revenue management, without the intervention of district or village *Zamindárs.*

Fifthly—In the disallowance of the farming system.

Sixthly—In the establishment of a Council of Ministers with their proper work allotted to them, and each directly responsible to the King in Council.

Seventhly—In the subordination of the Military to the Civil element in the administration.

Eighthly—In the intermixture of Bráhmans, Prabhus, and Maráthás in all offices, high and low, so as to keep check upon one another.

Of course some of these distinctive features could not be continued intact when the Maráthá power, instead of being confined to the small area of the *Swarájya* district, was extended in all directions so as to embrace provinces so distant as Katak on the East, and Káthiáwád on the West, Delhi in the North and Tanjore in the South. In the Maráthá country proper, the nation, the army, the officers, and the kings were all of the same race, and a common bond of loyalty knit them together in a way which it was impossible to secure in distant parts of India, where the conquered population differed essentially from the army of occupation, and too often the army of occupation consisted of mercenaries who had no bond of union with their commanding officers, or with the representatives of the central power. It is therefore not to be wondered at, that Shiváji's institutions, as described above, were not found elastic enough to be suitable for all parts of India. The connection of the hill-forts with the plains commanded by them, for instance, was a feature so entirely local that it could not be accepted as a practical basis of government in the plains of Gujarát or Málwá or in the Eastern Districts of Maháráshtra itself. For a similar reason, the strict system of direct revenue management and the total supercession of farmers and *Zamindárs* was also not equally suited for distant provinces where the traditions of government had been all along opposed to such direct collection. While therefore allowance may be made for these and other considerations, there can be no doubt that, in other respects, the departure from Shiváji's system was a distinctly retrograde step, for which no similar excuse can be pleaded, except that the men who came after did not realise the wisdom of his plans, and yielded to the temptation of present convenience, only to find that they had thereby lowered the organised union he had established into an unorganised mass held together by the very loosest ties, and threatening dissolution at the first great crisis in its history.

The system of Government by a Council of eight Ministers, for instance, was retained in the early years of Sháhu's reign, but gradually fell into disuse when the *Péshwá's* power increased so as to overshadow the other Ministers, and it actually ceased to exist when the *Péshwás* made Pooná their capital. The *Pant Amátya* and *Pant Sachiv*, the most powerful civil functionaries next to the *Péshwá*, occupy no place in the Maráthá history after Sháhu's death, and sank into the position of mere *Jahágirdárs*. The *Péshwás* did not venture or care to set up any substitute in their place, and presumed to manage all affairs on their own responsibility. They were their own generals, and their own finance ministers, and foreign ministers also. No wonder that the personal system of rule thus established had not the stability which it would have derived, if Shiváji's institutions had been faithfully respected by his successors.

The system of filling up high offices as though they were hereditary *vatans* was another retrograde departure from the instructions laid down by Shiváji, and systematically carried out by him. When the *Pêshwáship* itself became hereditary, it was not to be wondered at that every other office became hereditary also. But as natural capacity and virtues are not hereditary endowments, the office soon came to be filled up by incapable persons, and brought on sooner or later the expected disaster. Four generations of *Pêshwás* retained power by natural right, but the other officers had not even this claim to urge for the continuance of office in their families. New men rose from the ranks to the topmost positions, but there was no room for them in the general Councils of the Empire. Náná Fadnavis, for instance, from being a *Fadnavis*, aspired to be Prime Minister. Mahádaji Shindé, from being a *Sardár* of secondary importance, became the most powerful military commander of his time. There was no room for both of them and the like of them in the central Council, and each tried to supplant the other by force or craft, and each dragged the other down. More frequently still, the great military commanders became kings in their own territory, and made peace or war at their own will. This danger might have been, to a great extent, obviated, if the system of government by a Council, with the necessary enlargements dictated by altered circumstances, had been continued, and the hereditary principle not allowed to take such deep root, as it did in the course of two generations from Shiváji's death.

The greatest departure, however, was in the abandonment of the principle of not giving extensive territories as *jahágir* to those who could conquer them by the strength of their military prowess. To some extent this departure was forced upon the Government of Sháhu by the events that had preceded his accession to power. The whole country of Maháráshtra had been conquered by the Moghuls after Sambháji's death, and Sambháji's brother, Rájárám, and his Councillors had been driven far to the south. The whole work had to be commenced again, and the new leaders who came to power had to be allowed much their own way. No fault therefore can be laid at the door of Rájárám's advisers, and the stress and adverse circumstances continued to be in considerable strength in the early years of Sháhu. When, however, Sháhu's Government was established in Maháráshtra, and plans of extending the Empire in all directions were entertained, the temptation of present convenience was not so strong, and might have been resisted. It was just at this time that the mistake was committed of allowing every soldier of fortune to carve out his own *jahágir.* Piláji and Damáji Gáikawád settled themselves as sovereigns of Gujarát. The Bhonslés of Nágpur became supreme in those parts, while Shindé and Holkar and the Pavárs established themselves in Málwá and North India, under a very loose system of allegiance to the central power, represented by their agreement to pay a portion of the revenue to the *Péshwá* as wielding the chief authority in Maháráshtra. When these *jahágir* assignments were continued hereditary, the transformation from organized to unorganized power was complete. Those who first acquired these large domains retained some sense of loyalty to the common cause. Their successors, however, resented all interference with what they came to regard as their own private possessions. It was in this way that the more important departures from the policy laid down by Shiváji proved ruinous to the general interests.

Shiváji's arrangements about the direct management of land revenue, without the intervention of the district and village *Zamindárs*, were on the whole faithfully carried out by his successors, and during the best period of the *Péshwá's* rule, almost down to the death of Náná Fadnavis, the system of farming revenue found no favour. It was only under the rule of the last *Péshwá* that districts began to be farmed out in the Maráthá country proper. In the outlying conquests of Málwá, Gujarát and other parts of North India, the farming system was more in vogue, as being more suited to the unsettled condition of those parts. While in this matter, therefore, Shiváji's traditions were on the whole respected, the precautions he had taken about the distribution of offices amongst Maráthás, Bráhmans and Prabhus, do not appear to have commended themselves to his successors. The Prabhus, who had played such an important part in the early history of Shiváji, ceased to occupy any prominent place in the latter history of the *Péshwás* from Báláji Bájiráo's time. Only one great name, that of Sakhárám Hari, who was a favourite commander under Raghunáthráo Péshwá, appears in this later period, though in the Courts at Barodá and Nágpur, representatives of this class continued to play an important part as civil ministers and military commanders. As regards the Bráhmans, there is an impression that the Konkanastha section had no employment under the great Shiváji. The native chronicles, however, clearly show that Bráhmans of all the three sections of that community were employed as *Subhédárs* and Commanders of hill-forts. The Déshastha Bráhmans naturally took the lead in the times of Shiváji and his two sons. With the accession to power of the *Péshwás* in Sháhu's time, the balance was turned in favour of the Konkanasthas, and the disproportion became more manifest, because the leading Déshastha *Jahágirdárs* had taken the side of Raghunáthráo in his wars with his nephews.

The military profession had not been monopolised by the Maráthás in Shiváji's time, but they constituted the chief strength of the army, both in the ranks and file. The Bráhman commanders under Shiváji were as brave in generalship as any Maráthá Commander. This continued to be the case under the early *Péshwás*. The greatest Maráthá Commanders were trained in the school of the first Bájiráo Péshwá. When the great Maráthá families, who served under Bájiráo, established themselves in distant provinces as virtual rulers, and became so powerful as to threaten the safety of central authority, it was an aim of state policy at Poona to create an equipoise of Bráhman Commanders in the South, and the Patwardhans and the Fadkés, the Rástés and the Gokhalés, rose to command, but they never could hold their own against the armies of positions of Shindé and Holkar. The rivalry thus set up, however, proved, among other causes, most harmful to the general interest.

It will thus be seen that in all the points in which the principles of government laid down by Shiváji were departed from by his successors, we can trace the causes of the weakness and decline of the Maráthá power, long before it came in conflict with British authority in India. That authority, when it obtained supremacy, gave its deliberate preference to the principles laid down by Shiváji over those which found favour with his successors. British rule in India is carried on on the principle of enforcing a complete separation of the Civil from the Military department and a due subordination of the latter to the former. It insists upon cash payments for services rendered, and declines to make grants of lands by way of assignment for military or other services. It refuses to recognise any hereditary claims to public offices, high or low. The government is carried on by Boards and Councils, and not by the unfettered discretion of a single ruler. It collects its land revenue by its own paid agency, and never farms it out to the old *Zamindárs* or farmers. It also provides for a due distribution of offices among all classes of its subjects. As a consequence of the observance of these maxims of state policy, a handful of Englishmen have been able to govern the whole country in a way that strikes both native and foreign students of its administration as a marvellous feat of statesmanship. The wisdom of Shiváji's principles has been thus vindicated, not only by the success which he himself achieved, but by the success which has attended the efforts of those who built their power upon the ruins of the confederacy which he had tried to knit together, and which broke up chiefly because Shiváji's successors departed from the lines of policy laid down by him for their guidance.

CHAPTER VIII.

THE SAINTS AND PROPHETS OF MAHÁRÁSHTRA.

SAINT RÁMDÁS, the spiritual adviser of the great Shivâji, is reported to have exhorted Shiváji's son, Sambháji, to follow the footsteps of his father, and the advice he gave on this occasion was tersely summed up in two sentences—"Unite all who are Maráthás together," and "Propagate the *Dharma* (religion) of Mahárashtra." The first advice represents the leading feature of the political movement which assumed its final shape under Shiváji's leadership, and the second points no less clearly to the religious development which was at the same time going on all over the country, and of which the political movement was itself only a reflection. The point naturally arises for consideration—what Rámdás could have meant by recommending this second feature of Shiváji's policy, and exhorting Sambháji to propagate, not the *Vedic*, *Puránic*, or the Hindu religion generally, but the religion of Maháráshtra. What was there so particular and distinct in the religious belief of his contemporary countrymen which so strikingly attracted Rámdás's notice, and was deemed by him to be a sure remedy for securing the salvation of his people under the terrible misgovernment of Sambháji about the close of the seventeenth century ? The close connection between the religious and political upheaval in Maháráshtra is a fact of such importance, that to those who, without the help of this clue, have tried to follow the winding course of the growth of Maráthá power, the purely political struggle becomes either a puzzle, or dwindles down into a story of adventures, without any abiding moral interest. Both European and Native writers have done but scant justice to this double character of the movement, and this dissociation of the history of the spiritual emancipation of the national mind accounts for much of the prejudice which still surrounds the study of the Maráthá struggle for national independence.

We propose accordingly in this chapter to trace in rough outline the history of this religious upheaval in Western India.

Our main sources of information will be the voluminous biographies of the saints and prophets of Mahárāshtra, written by one of our own poets, Mahipati, towards the close of the last century, long before British influence was felt in these parts as a factor of any importance. Like the political struggle for independence, the religious upheaval was also not the work of a single man, or even of a single century. Its early commencement can be traced even anterior to the Mahomedan conquest of the Deccan. Under the rule of the Yádav kings of Dévgiri, Dnyándév, the first saint and prophet of Mahárāshtra, wrote his famous commentary on the *Bhagavatgitá* in the spoken language of the country. Mukundráj, who lived under the Ballál Kings, also wrote his famous work, the first of the kind in Maráthi in the twelfth century. The Mahomedan invasions for a time seem to have paralyzed all activity, but gradually the national spirit regained its healthy elasticity, and just about the time of the rise of the Maráthá power we had a galaxy of saints and prophets, whose names have become household words with the people of the country. The stream continued to flow in full tide for two centuries, and then it appears to have dried up, and with its ebb, the political domination also became a thing of the past. Roughly speaking we may state that the history of this religious revival covers a period of nearly five hundred years, and during this period some fifty saints and prophets flourished in this land, who left their mark upon the country and its people so indelibly as to justify Mahipati in including them in his biographical sketches. A few of these saints were women, a few were Mahomedan converts to Hinduism, nearly half of them were Bráhmans, while there were representatives in the other half from among all the other castes, Maráthás, *kunbis*, tailors, gardeners, potters, goldsmiths, repentant prostitutes, and slave girls, even the outcaste *Mahárs*. Much of the interest of this religious upheaval is centred in the facts we have noticed above, as they indicate plainly that the influence of higher spirituality was not confined to this or that class, but permeated deep through all strata of society, male and female, high and low, literate and illiterate, Hindu and Mahomedan alike. These are features which the religious history of few other countries can match or reproduce, unless where the elevating influence is the result of a widespread popular awakening. In

Northern and Eastern India a similar movement manifested itself much about the same time. Nának stirred up the Punjáb to rise, and made a supreme effort to reconcile Hinduism with Mahomedanism. Chaitanya in the far East sought to bring men back from the worship of *Shakti* and *Káli* to the faith of the *Bhagawat*; while Rámánand and Kabir, Tulsidás and Surdás, Jayadév and Rohidás, contributed each in his own way to the work of spiritual enlightenment. Their influence has no doubt been great and abiding, but it cannot be compared with the work done by the saints and prophets of Maháráshtra. The names of Chángdév and Dnyándév, Nivritti and Sopán, Muktábái and Jani, Ákábái and Vénubái, Námdév and Eknáth, Rámdás and Tukárám, Shaik Mahomed and Shánti Bahámani, Dámáji and Udhav, Bhánudás and Kurmdás, Bodhlé Báwá and Santobá Powár, Késhav Swámi and Jayarám Swámi, Narasinha Saraswati and Rangnáth Swámi, Chokhámélá and the two potters, Narahari Sonár and Sávatiá Máli, Bahiram Bhat and Ganésh Náth, Janárdanpant and Mudhopant, and many others that might be cited, furnish an array which testifies to the superior efficacy of this movement in Maháráshtra. The Bráhmans in these parts furnished a much larger proportion of saints and prophets than was the case in any of the other parts of India where the *Kshatriya* and *Vaishya* castes furnished a much larger contingent than the Bráhmans.

As is the case with all biographies of saints, the popular imagination attributes to these persons wonderful and miraculous powers, notably those of raising the dead to life, healing the sick and feeding the hungry. The stories which are told of the way in which they were helped by supernatural agency in their mission of love may or may not be accepted in these days of vigilant criticism. As Mr. Lecky has remarked, it is the atmosphere of child-like credulity which predisposes men to require and accept these wonders and miracles as events of ordinary occurrence. The saints and prophets themselves did not claim miraculous powers. They were meek and suffering men who placed their trust in Providence, and their trust was justified beyond their expectations, often-times to their own surprise. The moral interest of these biographies centres, however, not in their miraculous feats, but in their struggles, and in the testimony their lives afforded in vindication of the eternal verities of the moral law and man's higher spiritual life. It is with this aspect of their life that we are more immediately concerned in the sequel, and we hope to show that in this respect the work they accomplished was priceless and blessed beyond all comparison.

There is a curious parallel between the history of the Reformation movement in Western Europe and the struggle represented by the lives and teachings and writings of these saints and prophets who flourished about the same time in Mahárâshtra. The European reformers of the sixteenth century protested strongly against the authority claimed by the priests and the clergy with the Roman Bishop at their head. The clergy and the Pope represented a tradition of authority which had come down from the remote past, and had done signal service in its own time in humanizing and civilizing the hordes of the barbarian conquerors who devastated the Roman provinces. In course of time, the priests, instead of being the servants, claimed to be masters and rulers, with temporal and spiritual powers, and intermediaries between God and man. The exercise of this intercession was hedged round by numberless rites and ceremonies, and in course of time many abuses crept in and alienated general sympathy. These abuses assumed their worst forms about the time that Luther rebelled against the authority which issued indulgences and levied Peter's Pence, not as charity, but as a tax to subserve the temporal power of intriguing Popes and their vicious cardinals. The Reformation in Western India had its counterpart in this respect. Ancient authority and tradition had been petrified here, not in an ambitious Bishop and his clergy, but in the monopoly of the Bráhman caste, and it was against the exclusive spirit of this caste domination that the saints and prophets struggled most manfully to protest. They asserted the dignity of the human soul as residing in it quite independently of the accidents of its birth and social rank. The circumstances of their own birth and education naturally predisposed some of these preachers to take up such a position. As observed above, nearly half of them were of castes other than Bráhmans, and some of them of very low castes indeed. Many of the Bráhman reformers also had some stain in their inherited purity which led or forced them to rebel against all artificial restraints. Dnyándév and his brothers and sister Muktábái were born to their father after he had retired from the world and become a *Sanyási* monk. His spiritual guide, Rámánand, came to know that this *Sanyási* had not obtained his wife's willing consent to a change of *Áshram*, and he ordered him to go back to his native place and live with his wife. The children so born to the *Sanyási* became marked objects of caste aversion, and the Bráhmans refused to perform the initiation ceremony when the brothers reached the proper age. The children remained in this unrecognised condition all their life, and were revered notwithstanding this defect in their caste respectability. Another saint, Málopant, was married to a low-caste girl, whose caste was not discovered till after the marriage, and the husband did not abandon her, but only held no intercourse with her, and, when on her death, he performed her death-rites as usual, a miracle was displayed which satisfied his worst enemies, that Málopant and his *Mahár* wife were both holy by nature. Jayarám Swámi's master, Krishnadás, was similarly married to a barber girl, and the inferiority of her caste was discovered after marriage. The holy life of the man had, however, such an effect that at last, after much persecution, even the high priest Shankarácharya of the day raised no objection. Eknáth, it is well known, made no secret of the little importance he attached to caste distinctions. He fed an hungry *Mahár* at his house, and, when out-casted, allowed himself to be taken to the river for purposes of purification, when a miracle took place by which the merit of feeding an hungry *Mahár* was proved to be far greater than that of feeding many hundred Bráhmans, for the former merit cured a leper of his foul disease, when the latter failed to make any impression on him. A very common miracle is reported to have been performed by many of the saints notably by Dnyándév, Eknáth, and Nágnáth, when, on the refusal of the Bráhmans to officiate on *Shráddha* ceremonies in their places for breach of caste regulations, the deceased fathers of the obstinate Bráhmans were made to descend to earth, and shamed their incredulous sons into the belief that their caste exclusiveness was wholly out of place. In Námdév's biography, his God of Pandharpur, who had allowed Námdév to invite Bráhmans to a feast and himself partook of that feast with the saint, was himself excommunicated, and then the story relates how Dnyándév, who was present in spirit, remonstrated with the Bráhman persecutors.

He said :—"There was none high or low with God. All were alike to him. Never entertain the thought that I am high born, and my neighbour is low of birth. The Ganges is not polluted, nor is the wind tainted, nor the earth rendered untouchable, because the low born and high born bathe in the one, or breathe the other, or move on the back of the third."

The most touching incident, however, is that which occurred in the persecution of the out-caste *Mahár* Chokhámélá for his having dared to enter the temple of Pandharpur. When remonstrated with for his temerity, Chokhámélá replied that his God took him inside by force, and he did not go of his own accord. He remonstrated with the Bráhman worshippers of the temple in this strain—"What availeth birth in high caste, what availeth rites or learning, if there is no devotion, or faith? Though a man be of low caste, yet if he is faithful in heart, and loves God, and regards all creatures as though they were like himself, and makes no distinction between his own and other peoples' children, and speaks the truth, his caste is pure, and God is pleased with him. Never ask a man's caste when he has in his heart faith in God, and love of men. God wants in his children love and devotion, and he does not care for his caste." The Bráhmans, as might be expected, were not converted by this preaching of high wisdom, and they complained to the Musalman officer of the place, and he, like another Pilate of the Bible story, ordered Chokhámélá to be punished by being tied to and driven by a team of bullocks, and tortured to death in this cruel fashion. God, however, miraculously delivered his worshipper, and baffled the oppressors, for the bullocks would not move from their place. The story of Bahiram Bhat is also interesting in this connection. Being a *Shástri*, he did not find rest in Bráhminism, and therefore became a Mahomedan under the impression that its monotheism would satisfy the cravings of his heart, but failing to find the satisfaction he desired, he returned back to Bráhminism. Both Bráhmans and Mahomedans found fault with him for these changes of faith, but he disclaimed being either Hindu or Mohomedan. Bahiram Bhat challenged the Bráhmans to make him a true Bráhman as long as his circumcision mark was not removed, and he challenged the Mahomedans to fill up the holes in his ears, which showed that he was still a Hindu. The Mahomedan converts to Hinduism, represented by Shaik Mahomed's followers, even to this day observe the *Ramján* fasts, and the *Ekádashi* fast, and make pilgrimages to Mecca as also to Pandharpur. There are many other saints of great renown who, like Kabir, Nának and Mánik Prabhu are claimed both by Hindus and Mahomedans as belonging to their respective communities, and worshipped and reverenced as such by both. These examples will suffice to show how the lives of these men have tended to elevate the national conception of man's spiritual nature, and shake the hold of caste intolerance.

The result of all this elevated teaching is seen in the fact that caste exclusiveness now finds no place in the religious sphere of life, and it is relegated solely to the social concerns of men, and even there its restrictiveness is much relaxed, as any one can judge who compares the Bráhmans of Southern India with their exclusive caste prejudices, and their abhorrence of even the shadow of the lower castes defiling Bráhman streets, with the comparative indifference shown in such matters in the Deccan portion of Mahárástra. This feeling of indifference is most accentuated at the times of the annual pilgrim gatherings, and the mixed greetings with which the Lord's Feast is celebrated on the last day. Just as in Europe, men ceased to believe that the priest was a necessary medium between God and man for purposes of salvation, in this part of India, the domination of the Bráhman caste as the Gods of creation, whom the other castes should serve and worship, lost much of its potency, and men and women, high and low, came to feel that they were free to attain salvation by faith and love in spite of their low origin.

The European reformers protested further against the institution of the monastic orders, and the celibacy of the clergy, and the unnatural retirement of women who exiled themselves from the world and became nuns. There was a counterpart of this same protest in the way in which our saints and prophets raised their voice against self-mortification and fasts, and meaningless penances and endless pilgrimages. The same spirit prompted them to condemn austerities practised by those who followed the *Yoga* system with a view of acquiring the power of working wonders which, it was supposed, the *Yogis* enjoyed in consequence. This contest between *Yoga* and *Bhakti* is well illustrated by the encounter of the proud Chángdév with Dnyándév, when the former, in reliance on his *Yoga* powers, rode on tigers, and used serpent whips, and was put to shame by Dnyándév riding on a wall. There was a similar encounter between Dnyándév and Námdév when the former, by the exercise of *Yoga* powers, became small in size, and drank the waters of a deep well, while Námdév, by his devotion, brought the waters to overflow the well for all time, so that all who passed by, and felt thirsty, might drink to their hearts' content. These stories most beautifully typify this feature of the teaching of the saints and prophets of Maháráshtra.

The story of Kánobá Páthak, who was upbraided by a Bráhman of Benares for his inordinate love of children, and astonished his critic by throwing away his child into a well with seeming indifference, illustrates the vanity of the vows of celibacy, which cannot by themselves produce equableness of mind, and indifference to pains and pleasures. Eknáth all his life lived with his wife and children, and so did

Turkárám and Námdév, though they were not blessed with sympathetic female relations. Bodhlé Báwá, Chokhámélá, Dámájipant, Bhánudás, the two potter saints, and many others lived in the midst of their families. Dnyándév's father, who had become *Sanyási* without obtaining the free consent of his wife, was directed by Rámánand to return to his home, and live with his wife. All these incidents prove that a very high conception of the sanctity of family-life was realised by these saints and prophets, and they did their best to correct the national weakness which shrinks from trouble and anxiety by retiring from the world's conflict. The lives of the female saints have a special interest in this connection. The biographies relate that owing to their devotion and implicit faith, God helped them out of their difficulties by assisting them in their daily household work, and by assuming strange disguises, permitted them the freedom they wanted to serve him without being missed by their jealous relations. There is a danger in all such stories of making Providential intervention too cheap, but this fault is more than balanced by the high moral which underlies these accounts. The sanctity of married and family life was nobly vindicated by these saints and prophets, and this was a signal moral triumph over the past traditions of asceticism.

All students of modern European history are aware that the Reformers achieved their most permanent success in the liberation of the national intellect from the thraldom of scholastic learning, and the oppressive preponderance of the classical Latin in which all the best books were till then written. The Bible was, by the help of these Reformers, for the first time made accessible to all, high and low, and the monopoly of learning, till then enjoyed by the priests, was shaken to its foundations. Here in India, the process of liberation was carried out on the same lines. The professors of the old Sanskrit learning found for the first time to their great surprise that the saints and prophets addressed the people, both in speech and writing, in their own vernacular, and boldly opened the hitherto hidden treasures to all and sundry, men and women, Bráhmans and Shudrás, alike. The final victory was not achieved without much struggle and considerable suffering. Dnyándév was the first adventurer to stray into these forbidden regions, and his example was followed by

Eknáth and Rámdás, Námdév and Tukárám, Váman Pandit and Muktéshwar, Shridhar and Moropant. These last four gifted men are more celebrated as authors and poets than as religious teachers, but they derived their inspiration from the same sources. It is true the *Védás* and the *Shástrás* were not translated as the Bible was, but there was a sufficient reason for this difference. These early Marathi writers knew that modern India, after the Buddhistic revolution, was less influenced by the *Védás* and *Shástrás* than by the *Rámáyan* and *Mahábhárat*, the *Bhágawat Purán* and the *Gitá*, and these latter works were translated and made accessible to all. The pioneers in this field, Eknáth and Tukárám, were each made to bear the brunt of Bráhman opposition. Their works were not burned as in Europe, but they were ordered to be thrown into water. The river gods, however, so the story runs, would not let them be destroyed, and the works remained dry and would not sink, and thus became more famous than ever. Váman Pandit, the great Sanskrit scholar, who would not deign to speak or write in the popular language, as unfit to be used by a Pandit, was, when brought in contact with Rámdás, made to see the error of his ways; and a Bráhman translator of the *Rámáyan* named Sâlyâ Rasâl, who was over-proud of his superior learning, was similarly put to shame by a message from his goddess that he should get the work corrected by submitting it to the revision of the tailor Námdév. Dnyándév also was made the instrument of performing a miracle, by which a buffalo was said to have recited the *Védas* by heart. This story is obviously an allegorical parody of the mental condition of those who prided themselves upon their ability to recite the *Védas* without understanding their contents.

The struggle between the claims of the classical Sanskrit and the vernaculars, of which we hear so much in these days, is thus an old conflict, the issues in which were decided in favour of the vernacular or living languages long ago, and whatever scholars and antiquarians may urge to the contrary, there can only be one answer to the question,—the answer which was given by the saints and prophets when they laid Sanskrit aside as useless for their work, and spent all their energies in the cultivation and growth of their mother tongue. It may safely be said that the growth of the modern vernaculars in India is solely the result of the labours of these saints, and that the provinces, which showed most decided tendencies in the way of reform, also showed the most healthy development of their vernacular literature.

The Protestant reformers in Europe achieved another change of great importance in the way in which they raised their voice against the excesses to which image-worship and saint-worship were carried in the Roman Catholic Church. On our side, also, this protest was raised, but it did not assume the iconoclastic form which the Protestant reformers, especially the stricter sect among them, adopted. Polytheistic worship was condemned both in theory and in practice by the saints and prophets of Maháráshtra. Each of them had his own favourite form of the divine incarnation, and this worship of one favourite form left no room for allegiance to other gods. Rámdás, for instance, worshipped God under the name of Ráma; Ekanáth and Jayarám Swámi worshipped Him under the name of Krishna; Tukárám, Chokhámélá and Námdév under the name of Vithobá; Narahari Sonár and Nágnáth under the name of Shiva; Janárdan Swámi and Narasinha Saraswati under the name of Dattátraya; Moryá Gosávi and Ganéshnáth under the name of Ganapati, and so on for the rest. Strange stories are told in these biographies of the way in which the saints when they visited other shrines refused to see the image in the form in which they did not worship God, and as a consequence the image manifested itself to them in the form familiar to them. The supremacy of one God, one without a second, was the first article of the creed with every one of these saints, which they would not allow any body to question or challenge. At the same time, as observed above, the iconoclastic spirit was never characteristic of this country and all the various forms in which God was worshipped were believed to merge finally into one Supreme Providence or *Bramha*. This tendency of the national mind was a very old tendency. Even in Védic times, Indra and Varun, Marut and Rudra, while they were separately invoked at the sacrifices offered for their acceptance, were all regarded as interchangeable forms of the one and supreme Lord of creation. This same tendency explains the comparative indifference with which the saints and prophets treated the question of image-worship. It is a complete misunderstanding of their thoughts and ideas on this subject when it is represented that these gifted people were idolaters in the objectionable sense of the word. They did not worship stocks and stones. In Védic times there was admittedly no idol or image worship. It came into vogue with the acceptance of the incarnation theory, and was stimulated by the worship of the Jains and Buddhists of their saints. Finally, it got mixed up with fetish worship of the aboriginal tribes, who were received into the Áryan fold, and their gods were turned into incarnations of the Áryan deities. The saints and prophets, however, rose high above these grovelling conceptions prevalent amongst the people. Idol worship was denounced when the image did not represent the supreme God. Both Tukárám and Rámdás have spared no words in denouncing these aboriginal and village gods, and their frightful rites and sacrifices. In the life of Bhánudás, it is stated that he told the king of Vidyánagar that the Goddess he worshipped served his God at Pandharpur in a menial capacity as a sweeper, and the king found it to be the truth when he visited Pandharpur. In the lives of two other saints it is stated that the Goddess Káli, to whom human and animal sacrifices were offered, was so frightened by the protest of the saints in the name of Hari against such cruelty, that the sacrifices were given up by the command of the Goddess not only for the time, but for all time. These illustrations will serve to show, in what light image-worship, as an aid to devotion, was utilized by these saints, and unless this distinction is borne in mind, it will be impossible to understand the true position occupied by these teachers in this important matter.

There is one point, however, in which the reforming saints and prophets in this country differed essentially from those who were working in the same cause elsewhere, the contemporary Protestant reformers in Europe. From the Védic times downwards, the *Áryan* gods have been gods of love and of brightness, of sweetness and of light. There were, of course, terrible gods also, such as Varun and Rudra who inspired awe and filled the mind with terror. But the national tendency was to dwell with affection on and contemplate chiefly the bright side of divine Providence, unlike the Shemitic idea which dwelt upon the terrific manifestation of a distant god whose glory could not be seen save through a cloud, a severe chastiser of human frailties, and a judge who punished more frequently than He rewarded, and even when He rewarded kept the worshipper always in awe and trembling. This conception lies at the root of all Shemitic religions, and it is to the credit of Christianity that it attempted and partly succeeded in bridging the gulf by securing the intervention of God incarnate in the flesh, as Jesus Christ, who suffered for mankind, and atoned for their sins. This intervention was never found necessary in the *Áryan* religions of Greece or Rome or of India. God with us has always been regarded more as a father and a mother, a brother and a friend, than a judge and a chastiser and a ruler. Not that He does not judge, or rule, but He judges, rules, and chastises with the love of a father or mother, ever ready to receive the repentant prodigal son back into his arms. The orthodox Bráhminical conception does not bring out this feature of a kindly Providence so prominently as it is found to be realised in the teachings and life's experiences of our saints and prophets. They are emphatic in their assertions that they were able to see their God, and hear His words, and walked and talked with Him, and held intercourse with Him. In their higher moments they, no doubt, describe Him as One Who did not speak, but their most normal condition of mind was one of satisfaction when they realised His presence as we realise the presence of sensible things. The *Yogis* and the *Védántis* only talk in their waking dreams of being one with God, but Námdév and Tukárám, Eknáth and Dnyándév, were not content with this distant and difficult union, which did not last during all the moments of their conscious life, and compared their own happiness in such daily intercourse with God as being above all the attainments of *Yoga* and *Védánt*. We may believe the miracles ascribed to these saints or disbelieve them, but we cannot disbelieve their emphatic statements on this point. All the love that in Christian lands circles round the life and death of Christ Jesus has been in India freely poured upon the intense realisation of the every-day presence of the Supreme God in the heart in a way more convincing than eyes or ears or the sense of touch can realise. This constitutes the glory of the saints, and it is a possession which is treasured up by our people, high and low, men and women, as a solace in life beyond all value.

As a consequence of this conception of God's relations with man, the supreme efficacy of devotional love (*Bhakti*) over all other methods of attaining to His knowledge became the cardinal creed of these *Vaishnav* sects. There is not a life in all these sketches drawn by Mahipati in which *Bhakti* and Faith (*Bháwa*) are not emphasized as being far superior in virtue to all other forms of worship, such as the performance of rites and ceremonies of external worship, pilgrimages and ablutions, self-mortifications and fasts, learning and contemplation. These have relation only to the body or the mind, while the spirit is what God desires to see engaged in His service. The rites and ceremonies may be performed as in different matters, just as food may be taken and thirst quenched, and the rest of sleep enjoyed, as they come naturally without effort or unnecessary anxiety about them. The best ablution is when the senses are drowned in the ocean of God's presence about us, and the same presence is made to fill us inside and out. The best sacrifice and the highest *Dána* or gift is when we surrender ourselves to His sweet will and for His service, and claim nothing as our own. The best mortification is that which makes the spirit humble before Him; the best contemplation is when His glory is sung with all our powers. Neither knowledge nor *Yoga* powers, health nor wealth, nor children nor possessions, not even *Mukti* (freedom from birth and death), is desirable in itself. What is desirable is to be always full of love for Him and His works, including all creation, men and animals. Námdév cried while removing the bark of a tree, because he thought he saw blood coming out from the stroke of his axe, and he struck himself with the axe to see how he felt, and realise what the tree might feel. Shaik Mahomed, being sent by his father to practise the butcher's trade, first cut his own finger with his knife to see how the animal would feel, and the pain he felt drove him to forswear his trade, and retire from the world in which such pain had to be inflicted for earning one's livelihood. Tukárám felt that there must be something wrong about him, when, on seeing him, the sparrows left the field he was sent to watch, though he did not intend to disturb them. This intense spirituality and absolute surrender of self may sound somewhat unreal to men not brought up in the atmosphere these saints breathed. But there can be no doubt about the fact, and there can also be no doubt that the national ideal of spiritual excellence has been shaped by these models. It may be that a stronger backbone and more resisting power are needed in the times in which we live, but in an account of the saints and prophets as they flourished more than two hundred years ago, we cannot afford to interpolate our own wants and wishes.

It may be interesting to note how these saints thought and spoke, and how, when they came in contact with a militant religion like Mahomedanism, they faced their troubles and conquered them. The lives of Námdév, Rámdás, Eknáth, and others are full of such incidents. The most noteworthy fact in this connection is that several Mahomedans became converts to the Hindu Faith, and obtained such a public recognition that their help was invoked by the Hindu authors who wrote in those times along with the Hindu saints. Shaik Mahomed and Kabir may be cited as examples of this catholic spirit of recognition. On the other hand, Tukárám and Eknáth were so influenced by their contact with Mahomedanism that they composed verses in Urdu of so catholic a character as to be unobjectionable to the strictest Mahomedan. Rámdás did the same when one of his disciples, Udhav, got into trouble at Bédar. The story of Dámájipant, a servant of the Bédar Kings, is well known to all. In a time of famine he distributed the Government stores of grain among the poor, and on being taken to task he was relieved by an unexpected remittance of the full value of the grain to the King's treasury. The saints came out well in their struggles with their foreign rulers, and they prevailed not by fighting nor by resistance, but by quiet resignation to the will of God. There was a tendency perceptible towards a reconciliation of the two races in mutual recognition of the essential unity of Allá with Ráma, and by the time Shiváji appeared on the scene, this reconciliation seems to have been almost complete, though occasional outbursts of Mahomedan fanaticism were not altogether unknown even then.

We have thus noticed all the principal features of the religious movement, which, commencing with Dnyándév who lived in the fifteenth century, can be traced to the end of the last century as a steady growth in spiritual virtues. It gave us a literature of considerable value in the vernacular language of the country. It modified the strictness of the old spirit of caste exclusiveness. It raised the *Shudra* classes to a position of spiritual power and social importance, almost equal to that of the Bráhmans. It gave sanctity to the family relations, and raised the status of woman. It made the nation more humane, at the same time more prone to hold together by mutual toleration. It suggested and partly carried out a plan of reconciliation with the Mahomedans. It subordinated the importance of rites and ceremonies, and of pilgrimages and fasts, and of learning and contemplation, to the higher excellence of worship by means of love and faith. It checked the excesses of polytheism. It tended in all these ways to raise the nation generally to a higher level of capacity both of thought and action, and prepared it, in a way no other nation in India was prepared, to take the lead in re-establishing a united native power in the place of foreign domination. These appear to us to be the principal features of the religion of Maháráshtra, which Saint Rámdás had in view when he advised Shiváji's son to follow in his father's footsteps, and propagate this faith, at once tolerant and catholic, deeply spiritual and yet not iconoclastic.

CHAPTER IX.

GINGI.

FEW people, even in his own days, realized the gravity of the second great crisis in Maráthá History, which the untimely death of Shiváji precipitated in the Deccan. The first crisis occurred when Shiváji agreed to surrender unconditionally to Rájá Jayasing, and went to Delhi, where he was made prisoner by the Emperor. His genius and his good fortune enabled him not only to effect his escape, but to secure from Aurangzéb himself a recognition that he was a power in the land to be conciliated at any cost, till he could be crushed. Shiváji was well aware of Aurangzéb's designs on the Deccan, and the last twelve years of his life were devoted to the sole purpose of preparing the country to receive and repel the final blow. Forgetting internecine quarrels with the Mahomedan kingdoms in the South, Shiváji persuaded the kings of Bijápur and Golcondá to enter into offensive and defensive alliances with himself, and both these kingdoms profited by his help in repelling the attacks of the Moghul generals and consented to pay him tribute in recognition of his services. As if he had prescience of coming events, Shiváji, by his conquests and alliances, formed a new line of defence in Southern India in the Kávéri valley, to which he could retire in case of necessity. The hill forts along the Sahyádri Gháts and mountain ranges were kept in a state of repair, and the naval armaments under his commanders were his second line of defence. Above all, the men whom he had trained by a long course of discipline to follow him wherever he led them, and even to anticipate his wishes with unerring loyalty and success, the spirit of independence he had roused in all classes, and the faith he had inspired in them—these were the chief supports of the power, which was, by the confession of friends and foes alike, supreme in Southern India. His death was sudden as well as premature, for he had no time to make proper arrangements for regulating the succession to his kingdom. His eldest son had grossly misbehaved and disobeyed his orders and gone over to the protection of the Moghul generals. On his return from the Moghul camp, Sambháji was kept a close prisoner at Panhálá. The ministers at

Ráigad knew that Sambháji was unfitted, by his character and habits, to carry on the task which Shiváji had begun, and they contrived to set him aside and to place the younger son, Rájárám, on the throne. The Ráigad ministers in their haste committed the unfortunate mistake of not taking the army into their confidence. The Sénápati Hambirráo Mohité was not in their secret, and the plot failed in consequence. With the help of the army, Sambháji succeeded in effecting his escape from Panhálá and, overcoming the opposition of the ministers at Ráigad, obtained possession of the *gádi*. The cruel use he made of his success indicated his utter unfitness to be the leader of the nation in the coming crisis. He killed his own step-mother by starvation, imprisoned the old *Péshwá*, the old *Sachiva*, the old *Sumant* and killed the old Secretary of Shiváji's time. These cruelties continued all through his reign and he soon alienated the affections of all those who had risen to greatness under his father. Sambháji was naturally brave, and it seemed at one time as if, notwithstanding his cruelties, he would keep up the prestige of the Maráthá power in its wars with its neighbours. These promises were not realized. His excessive indulgence in drinking and debauchery soon unnerved him, and made him a slave to the most superstitious beliefs in witchcraft and demon-worship, under the advice of his favourite Kalushá. It is useless to enter into a detailed account of Sambháji's reign; for Sambháji never can be said to have ruled the country. The *Ashta Pradháns*, being virtually set aside, ceased to bear the responsibility of rule in Sambháji's time. The civil and military arrangements of his father were neglected, the soldiers were not paid regularly, the hill-forts were not properly garrisoned or provisioned, and district-revenues were farmed to the highest bidder. Anarchy prevailed everywhere, and it was just at this time that Aurangzéb descended into the Deccan with an army estimated at three lakhs of all arms, determined to crown the work of his life by the final subjugation of the Hindu and Mahomedan kingdoms in Southern India. The whole resources of Hindustán in men and money, from Kábul and Kandáhár on one side, to Bengal on the other, were requisitioned for this enterprise, and they were directed by his best Hindu and Mahomedan generals. Sambháji threw away a splendid opportunity, presented by one of the Emperor's sons, who sought refuge with him, to resist this new danger. He also resented all the efforts made by the old ministers to awake him to a sense of the danger that now threatened him. Aurangzéb's army conquered Golcondá and Bijápur within three years from his coming to the Deccan, and Sambháji was easily captured in a state of utter helplessness and subsequently beheaded with cruel indignity. All the plain country was over-run and the hillforts were taken one after another without struggle, chiefly because their defences had been neglected. At last Ráigad itself was captured, and Sambháji's wife and son were taken to Aurangzéb's camp. Aurangzéb's dream, which he cherished throughout his life, had thus been accomplished before he had been five years in the Deccan. The whole country from Narmadá to Tungabhadrá lay at his feet. It seemed as if Shiváji, and the men whom he had led to victory, had lived and died in vain. The great deluge, against which Shaháji and Shiváji had struggled to protect the country for over sixty years, now swept over the land, carrying everything before it, and there seemed no sign of any possible resistance. The old Bijápur and Golcondá rulers were captives in distant lands, and Sambháji's son was quite a boy of tender years and a prisoner in the camp.

But just when their country's fortune was at its lowest ebb, and everything seemed to be lost beyond hope, these very misfortunes served to rouse a band of patriots, who had been trained in Shiváji's school, to resolve—resourceless and penniless as they were—to secure their national independence, and drive Aurangzéb's grand army back to Hindustán. At the head of this band was Rájárám, the younger son of Shiváji, who had been kept a prisoner at Ráigad by Sambháji, and who, on Sambháji's death, effected his escape before Ráigad was captured. Rájárám was about twenty years old at this time, but he inherited most of the great qualities of his father—his daring and his skill, his freedom from vice, and the mildness and liberality of his disposition, and above all, his power of inspiring confidence among his countrymen. He professed all his life to act as Regent for Sháhu, who was a prisoner with Aurangzéb, and never sat on the throne out of respect for Sháhu's rights. The chief adviser of Rájárám on this occasion was Pralhád Niráji, the son of the *Nyáyádhish* Niráji Ráoji in Shiváji's time. During Sambháji's reign, Pralhád Niráji was out of office, and remained a passive spectator of affairs, but he was reputed to be the wisest man of the time among the Maráthás. Mr. Grant Duff, who is so sparing in his commendation of Bráhmans, admits that Pralhád was a very uncommon person, and, in his total disregard of self-interest, is almost a singular instance amongst Bráhman statesmen. Like Rájárám, Pralhád Niráji died, while the work of self-defence was but half-finished, but they both had the satisfaction of having lived to see that the danger which threatened their country was fairly mastered, and final success was only a question of time. Raghunáthpant Hanmanté was another of these patriots. He was the son of Shaháji's oldest Bráhman *kárkun* in charge of his *jahágir* in Karnátik, and was noted for his unselfishness and independence. He had vainly tried to advise Vénkoji at Tanjore and Sambháji at Ráigad to mend their ways, and now when the crisis came, he fell in with the plan of Pralhád Niráji, and prepared the fort of Gingi, which was in Shaháji's *jahágir* in the Tanjore District, to receive Rájárám and his partisans. Nilo Moréshwar, the son of the first *Péshwá* Moropant Pinglé, had been sent in advance to assume charge and complete the fortification of Gingi. Among the Bráhman leaders, whom it was determined to leave in the Deccan, and carry on a system of guerilla warfare, the most prominent man was Rámchandrapant Amátya, the ancestor of the present Pant Amátya family of Bávadá in Kolhápur. Rámchandrapant was a son of Abáji Sondév, who, with Moropant Pinglé, was, in Shiváji's time, his chief adviser and military commander. So great was the confidence placed in him that full authority was conferred upon him to act as circumstances required, and in his charge Rájárám left his wife, and most of the Maráthá commanders, who retreated to the South, placed their families under his protection at Vishálgad.

He was thus the chief ostensible authority, representing the Maráthá power, left in the Deccan, who did not submit to the Moghul Emperor. Another Bráhman leader, who deserves to be named, was Shankaráji Malhár, who was appointed *Sachiva* by Sambháji. He accompanied the leaders who went to Gingi, and after staying there for some time he retired to Benáres. He rendered a special service to Sháhu on his return to power by arranging the treaty between the Sayyads and the Maráthás. Among the Bráhman leaders, who rose to power for the first time in this crisis, was Parashurám Trimbak, the *Kulkarni* of

Kinhai, and the ancestor of the Pant Pratinidhi family of Oundh in Sátárá, as also Shankaráji Náráyan, the ancestor of the family of Pant Sachiva of Bhor. They were Rámchandrapant's chief assistants and nobly justified the confidence placed in them by their countrymen. Among the Maráthá leaders, the chief responsibility rested upon Santáji Ghorpadé and Dhanáji Jádhav. They had first come to notice as generals under Hambirráo Mohité, when they succeeded in turning a defeat into victory near Panhálá in 1674. For thirty years they maintained the reputation of the Maráthá arms, and braved the whole power of the Moghul army. Though they accompanied Rájárám, Pralhád Niráji and others to Gingi, the plan of defence settled upon was that they should return and oppose the Moghuls in the Deccan and prevent them from successfully invading the Karnátik and threatening Gingi. Of course, they were fighting without funds and without resources, and they had to improvise their own men, their horses, their supplies, ammunitions of war, and to find their treasure, and naturally many excesses were committed by them. They were fighting against the whole power of the Moghuls, and they established such a terror in the Moghul army that before the century came to an end, the Maráthás were able to return to their country and to make incursions in Gujarát, Málwá, Khándésh and Bérár, so as to reduce the Emperor's army to great straits. Santáji was killed by treachery by one of his private enemies, before the war of independence was closed, but his three brothers carried on the struggle with the Moghuls on their own accounts, and became the founders of small principalities at Gooty and Soondu. Dhanáji lived to see the final return of Sháhu to his own kingdom.

Among the other Maráthá leaders, Khandéráo Dábhádé occupies a prominent place. His father had been *Patel* of Talégáon and employed in Shiváji's service. He was one of those who accompanied Rájárám to Gingi, and was the first Maráthá leader to carry the war into the settled provinces of the empire, outside the Deccan, *viz.*, into Gujarát and Khándésh. One of his coadjutors, the founder of the Pawár family of Dhár and Dévás, entered Málwá. Khandéráo was one of those who lived long enough to accompany Báláji Vishwanáth when he went to Delhi to obtain the *sanads* of *chowth* and *sardéshmukhi* for Sháhu from the Delhi Emperor. Among the other Maráthá leaders who served with distircion in this war, we may mention the Áthawalé, Sidoji Náik Nimbálkar, Parsoji Bhonslé, founder of the Nágpur Rájá's kingdom, and Némáji Shindé. The Thoráts, Ghádgé, Thokés, Mahárnava, Pándharé, Kákdé, Pátankar, Bángar, Kadu, and other leaders were trained by the hard discipline of this long war to render eminent services to their country. Rájárám's advisers adopted the plan of authorising these partisan leaders to collect *chowth* and *sardéshmukhi* in the provinces subject to the Moghul authority. Parsoji Bhonslé thus obtained a *ṡanad* for collecting *chowth* in Gondvan and Bérárs. The Nimbálkars had Gangthadi assigned to them. The Dábhádés had charge of Gujarát and Khándésh, and the other leaders were quartered in Karnátik and the provinces recently conquered by the Moghuls.

Among the Prabhu leaders two deserve special mention. Though his father and uncle had been cruelly executed by Sambháji, Khando Ballál Chitnis, the son of Shiváji's Chief Secretary, Báláji Avji, remained faithful and was taken into favour by Sambháji by reason of his devotion in the wars with the Portuguese.

On Sambháji's death, he was one of those who accompanied Rájárám to Gingi, and when at Bélláry the Mahomedan governor was about to seize these fugitives in disguise, Khando Ballál at great self-sacrifice remained behind and sent away his other companion. He was seized by the Moghul governor and subjected to cruel torture, which, however, failed to shake him in his loyal devotion to the cause. Later on, he arranged for the safe escape of Rájárám from Gingi by coming to a friendly understanding with some Maráthá generals in the Moghul army, which understanding was secured by the surrender of his *vatan* in the Konkan to these Maráthá commanders. He lived to see the time when Sháhu returned to Sátárá and ascended his ancestral throne. Another Prabhu leader who covered himself with glory in these wars was Prayágji, who defended Sátárá against the besieging army led by Aurangzéb himself for months together.

These were the chief Bráhman, Maráthá and Prabhu patriot leaders, who, undaunted by the tide of adversity, determined to fight to the last for their national independence, and, being unable to find breathing-time for maturing their defensive arrangements in the Deccan, retired to the South and established themselves at Gingi. Rájárám appointed his own *Ashta Pradháns*, held his court there, and as if he was still master of his own country, gave *ináms* and *jahágirs* to those who had rendered eminent services and directed his commanders to carry on the war against the Moghuls with redoubled energy. Partisan leaders were also sent duly commissioned to raise their own forces and demand the *chowth* and *sardéshmukhi* not only in the six Deccan *subhás*, but also in the older provinces of the Moghul empire. Aurangzéb soon found that his conquest in the Deccan availed him nothing unless he crushed this new centre of power where the Maráthá leaders had retired. Zulfikarkhan, the conqueror of the Deccan, was accordingly sent to lay siege to Gingi, and he invested the place in 1691. But the place had been so well fortified, and Santáji Ghorpadé and Dhanáji Jádhav, who had the charge of harassing the Moghul besiegers, did their work so well that it was not till 1698 that Zulfikar was able to take the fortress, only to find that Rájárám and his men had made their escape. This seven years' period afforded the Maráthás the breathing time they stood in such sore need of, and trained them to measure their strength with the Moghuls on equal terms. The terror inspired by Aurangzéb's army was soon dispelled, and while Gingi was being defended by one portion of the Maráthá army, Dhanáji Jádhav and Santáji Ghorpadé returned to the Deccan and soon succeeded in bringing to the standard the veteran troopers, *Silédárs* and *Bárgirs*, of Shiváji's time. The exaction of *ghásdáná* was made on a system by which these unpaid and volunteer armies found their commissariat supplies. Even as early as 1691 Maráthá bands plundered Násik, Bede, and Bédar. In 1692 Rámchandrapant moved from Vishálgad and fixed his residence at Sátárá, and governed the Ghátmáthá country, and sent off an army which cut off the Moghul garrisons at detached places. Wái, Rájgad, Panhálá and Miraj were in this way captured and turned into Maráthá out-posts.

The Pawárs, Chaváns, Thoráts and Áthawalés earned distinction from the Court at Gingi by their success in partisan warfare. In 1693, Aurangzéb found it necessary to move his camp to the Bhima and sent his own son and chief minister Asudkhán to Gingi.

In 1694, the Maráthás under Santáji Ghorpadé plundered the country to the north of Aurangzéb's camp, and Rámchandrapant carried on the war in the west up to Solápur. In 1695, Santáji left Parsoji Bhonslé and Hayabatráo Nimbálkar in Bérár and Gangthadi to harass the Imperial convoys from Delhi, and himself proceeded to Karnátik, and attacked the besiegers in force, and routed them; while Dhanáji assisted Santáji in completing the disaster by a flank attack. The besiegers were thus rendered completely helpless; and a truce was arranged between the minister Asudkhán and Santáji, by which under certain conditions the Moghuls were to be allowed to retire. Aurangzéb, however, did not approve this conduct of his minister and recalled his son and sent a new army under Zulfikarkhán. The siege, however, was not renewed for some time. Meanwhile, Santáji, being free from immediate danger, hovered round the Emperor's camp at Bijápur and defeated his Governor Kasimkhán near *Doderi,* and Kasimkhán surrendered.

Another General Himatkhán was similarly entrapped and defeated. At last in 1697 the siege was renewed and, as stated above, after Rájárám had made his escape the Fort was taken in January 1698. Rájárám soon joined Rámchandrapant at Sátárá: and one by one the Maráthá generals, Parsoo Bhonslé, Hayabatráo Nimbálkar, Némáji Shindé, Áthawalé, Samshér Bahádur returned back to their country. The principal seat of the operation of the war was now transferred from the Karnátik and Dravid country to the Deccan, though Dhanáji Jádhav was still left in the South to defend the Maráthá possessions. The forts along the sea coast continued to be faithful to the Maráthá cause, and under Kánhoji Ángré the Maráthás carried on their depredations all along the coast from Trávancore to Bombay, capturing prizes at sea. The Sánvats also remained faithful.

In 1699, Rájárám at the head of all his army entered Khándésh, Gangthadi and Bérár and Báglan, and levied the *chowth* and *sardéshmukhi* in those parts. On his return to Sátárá he kept four of his commanders in those provinces permanently, Dabhádé in Báglan, Shindé in Khándésh, Bhonslé in Bérár, and Nimbálkar in Gangthadi.

In 1700, Aurangzéb determined to reduce the forts which proved so advantageous to the Maráthá plan of defence. He himself assumed the command of the army detached for this work and directed Zulfikarkhán to carry on the operations in the open country against Rájárám's army. Fort after fort was thus conquered, and finally he laid siege to Sátárá, which fell into his hands after a protracted and glorious defence conducted by Prayágji Prabhu. Just about this time Rájárám died at Sinhagad, and as Sháhu was still a prisoner in the Moghul camp, his elder son, a boy of ten years, was nominated successor, and Rámachandrapant conducted the administration as before. Dhanáji was recalled from the Karnátik, and the Maráthá leaders under his and Rámachandrapant's guidance continued the war with unabated vigour, levying *sardéshmukhi*, *chowth* and *ghásdáná* all over the country. The Emperor on his own side persisted in his plan of operation and stormed fort after fort during the next four years. It was a strange reversion in the plan of operations. Driven from their forts, the Maráthás spread over the plains invading Khándésh, Bérár, and Gujarát; and a party even crossed Narmadá into Málvá, and established themselves there. At last in 1705, Aurangzéb's military and civil advisers suggested to him that a treaty should be made with the

Maráthás ; and Aurangzéb was so far persuaded as to consent to the recognition of the claim for *sardéshmukhi* of the six Deccan *Subhás* on condition that the Maráthás were to be responsible for maintaining order in the Deccan. He also arranged for Sháhu's marriage with two ladies of the noble Maráthá families of Shindé and Jádhav who were in the Moghul service, and gave Shâhu Akkalkot, Indápur-Nivásé and Bárámati in *jahágir* as marriage-gift. These negotiations fell through because the Maráthás increased their demands. The war was carried on in a languid way on the part of the Moghuls, while the Maráthás re-took Pimalá and made it the residence of their king Shiváji and his mother Tárábái. Pávangad, Vasantgad, Sinhagad, Rájagad, and Sátárá were also retaken ; and, later on, Dhanáji retook Poona and Chákan in 1707. Aurangzéb was thus discomfited in all his plans, and with a view to create dissension among the Maráthás, he induced Sháhu to write a letter in his own name, as king of the Maráthás, to their leaders, advising them to submit to the Emperor. This was his last desperate resource and it proved ineffectual. Nothing was done in the way of Sháhu's release during Aurangzéb's lifetime ; but the overtures for peace and the letters addressed by Sháhu at his suggestion show that he was thoroughly satisfied that the war that had been waged for twenty years was a disastrous mistake on his part so far as the Maráthás were concerned. His splendid army had been disabled or killed, his own tent had been plundered, and he was himself in great danger of being captured; and it was not without reason that, when Aurangzéb came to die at Ahmednagar, he confessed that his life was a failure; and the poor Emperor died a broken-hearted penitent, weighed down with the wreck of all his hopes and ambition.

Soon after his death, Shâhu was released by his son Azimsháh with the advice of Zulfikarkhán, with a promise that, if he was accepted as king by the Maráthá leaders, the old territory, called *Swarájya*, conquered by his grandfather from Bijápur, would be restored to him with additional *jahágirs* between the Bhimá and the Godávari. Shâhu was accepted as king by the Maráthá leaders, and was crowned at Sátárá in 1708; and within a few years of that date he made himself master of the old possession of the Maráthá country with the exception of the district of Kolhápur which remained in the possession of Rájárám's son. The Moghul governor of the Deccan acknowledged Sháhu's claim to the *chowth* and *sardéshmukhi* over the six *Subhás*, and within the next ten years, Báláji Vishwanáth Péshwá and Khandéráo Dábhádé succeeded in obtaining the formal *sanads* for the *chowth*, the *sardéshmukhi*, and the *Swarájya*.

In this way, the twenty years' War of Independence was brought to a happy termination. Judging by the results achieved, there can be no doubt that these twenty years represent the most glorious period of Maráthá History. Shiváji had never to fight with the whole force of the Moghul Empire ; in fact, he actually made his submission to them at great self-sacrifice, when he was hard-pressed by their general Jayasing. He had, besides, the advantage of being able to count upon the support of two Mahomedan States in the South and to play them against the Moghul power. Lastly, he was fighting under the protection of his own hill-forts. In all these respects, the patriots who carried on the War of Independence to a successful issue were at great disadvantage. They had no leader, such as Shiváji, whose personal character and exploits had a magnetic power which none of his countrymen could resist. They had to fight with the whole of the Imperial army, led by Aurangzéb himself with all the resources of India at his command. Owing to Sambháji's cruelty and disorder, their most experienced leaders were killed, and their forts were unprepared for defence. Their prince was a prisoner in the hands of the Moghuls; and they were driven from home to take refuge in a foreign land. Without revenues, without armies, without forts, and without resources of any kind, they managed to raise armies, retake forts, and develop a system of conquest, by which they regained not only the *swarájya,* but also the right to levy *chowth,* and *sardéshmukhi* over the Deccan and the Karnátik. Many of the men, such as Rájárám, Pralhád Niráji, Santáji Ghorpadé and others, who conceived and carried out this plan of operations, died in the midst of the struggle; but their places were taken up by others with equal devotion and success. If Aurangzéb had not invaded the Deccan and forced on this war, it is just possible that a small principality might have been established in Western Maháráshtra like that at Tanjore, and the Moghul Emperor might have succeeded in counting upon its chief as one of his great nobles. The impulse, given by Shivájі, would have ceased to be operative in the second generation; the separatist tendency, always so powerful, would have again asserted itself, and the formation of the Maráthá nation would have been an impossibility.

If all these dangers were averted, and a new force communicated to the people, the credit of it must be ascribed to Aurangzéb's ambition. He stirred the people of Maháráshtra to their inmost depths; and it was the hard discipline of this twenty years' war, which cemented the national and patriotic instincts of their leaders, and during the next three generations carried them as conquerors to the farthest part of India. In this respect, the War of Independence did far greater service than even the struggle which Shivájі initiated and carried on during the whole of his chequered career. Mere freebooters and plunderers never could have obtained success in such a war against such a foe. It was a higher moral force which brought out all the virtues of the best men of the nation,—daring heroism, noble endurance, administrative skill, hope which rose higher with every disappointment, a faith which was never shaken, devotion to a high ideal which was independent of time, place, or person, a sense of brotherhood in common danger, a spirit of complete self-sacrifice and mutual concession for the common good, a trust in the final success of their cause, because it was the cause of their religion. These were the virtues which enabled the patriots of this generation to accomplish the deliverance of their country from a danger which no other race in India had been able to withstand. It is as a school for the teachings of these virtues and as a severe but a salutary discipline, that the War of Independence will ever be regarded as constituting the most eventful period of Maráthá History.

CHAPTER X.

HOW ORDER WAS BROUGHT OUT OF CHAOS.

THE close of the twenty years' war of National Independence secured, as stated in the last chapter, the liberation of Sháhu, and his return to the Deccan as the recognized leader of the Maráthás with a commission to carry out the policy of his grandfather Shiváji in organizing the union of Maháráshtra. Though the war may be said to have thus achieved the main objects for which it was waged against the armies of the Moghul Emperor, the fierce passions which had been aroused among the great partisan leaders, each of whom fought for his own hand, and was little disposed to give up his own independence, left behind a scene of confusion and chaos out of which for some years more it was found almost hopeless to evolve order in the country. The sentiment which had given a common purpose to the Maráthá leaders failed to animate them to work together as soon as Aurangzéb's death and the discomfiture of his armies removed the check on the dissociated patriots of the War of Independence. It would seem as if the return of Sháhu was intended by the advisers of the Emperor to serve a double purpose of creating dissension and strife among the Maráthás under the ostensible pretext of satisfying the national sentiment. Sháhu on his return was not welcomed by many of the partisans who had served under Rájárám, and espoused the cause of Tárábái and her son. The Pant Sachiv and the Pant Amátya held aloof from Sháhu, and the only distinguished leader of the old national party who left Tárábái's cause was Dhanáji Jádhav, who was sent to oppose Sháhu, but made common cause with him on being satisfied that his claim was just. Dhanáji Jádhav's great rival Santáji Ghorpadé had been cruelly attacked and killed by the Máné Déshmukhs of Mhaswad, and his three sons were struggling in the Karnátik to carry on the war against the Moghuls on their own account. Dhanáji Jádhav did not live long after Sháhu's return to power, and his son Chandrasén Jádhav was too self-willed to be controlled by the higher considerations which had kept his father at the head of the national armies in the War of Independence. On the pretext of a petty quarrel in a hunting expedition with the future Péshwá Báláji Viswanáth, he left his master's service, and after going over first to Kolhápur, finally joined the Nizám of Hyderábád, and his services were thus lost to the national cause. Among the other leaders, Khandéráo Dábhádé was strengthening himself in Khándésh with a view to further operations in Gujarát. Némáji Shindé, who was one of Rájárám's chief lieutenants, appears later on to have joined the Moghuls. Parsoji Bhonslé was like the Dábhádé carving out his fortunes in Bérár and Gondawana. Both Khandéráo Dábhádé and Parsoji Bhonslé, without sacrificing their independent careers, strengthened the hands of Sháhu by espousing his cause against Tárábái. Hayabatráo Nimbálkar, who had established himself in Gangthadi, was more dubious in his allegiance. On being displaced from power soon after, he left Sháhu's service, and joined the Nizám. The first class leaders were thus equally divided between Sháhu, Tárábái, and the service of the Nizám. Among the second class men, Kánhoji Ángré adhered to Tárábái's cause and had made himself master of the Konkan. The Thoráts, the Chaváns, and the Áthavalés were setting up independence for themselves. The first two were especially troublesome at the time when Sháhu ascended his grandfather's throne at Sátárá. They plundered on all sides, and as if in defiance of all traditions, they claimed their own dues of *chouth* and *ghásdáná* in mockery of the claims made by the central authority. A Bráhman freebooter who had been titled as a Mahárájá by the Moghul Governor, established himself at Khatáo within twenty miles of Sátárá, and thus reduced Sháhu's dominions to the confines of his own capital and a few hill-forts garrisoned by his own commandants.

This was the state of things which Sháhu's advisers had to face at the time of his accession to the throne. The marks of the war which had been concluded with such apparent success were visibly plain in the general unrest and disorder which it left behind. The power and the strength were still there, but without the animating spirit of a common purpose which held them together under the pressure of the war. Sháḥu had passed the best years of his life in confinement, and though latterly his confinement was not onerous, he had contracted the easy habits of the Mahomedan nobility among whom he had been brought up. He could not be expected to sympathise with the national hatred of the Moghuls which characterised his father and grandfather, and he was content to make his peace if allowed to rank as a great noble of the Moghul Empire. He had personal bravery and many good qualities of head and heart, but the organizing genius and the close application to work which alone could evolve order out of chaos had not been inherited by him from his grandfather. The Moghul governors were still in possession of all but a few hill-forts in the Deccan, and their armies though discomfited, were still able to command the field. Sháhu was not, under these circumstances, fitted by nature or temperament, to devise a scheme of policy, and achieve success by his own unaided efforts. None of his commanders also had the larger vision which the needs of the position at such a time demanded. During the first few years it seemed as if the plans of Zulfikarkhán were about to bear fruit. The Maráthás were able to make no impression collectively by reason of their being split up by mutual jealousy and misunderstandings. The great opportunity that had thus been presented, would have passed away if some master minds had not then come to the front, and fortunately for Sháhu, attracted his notice in the very first years of his accession to power. Mere force and daring did not represent the want of the time, there was more than enough of it. What was needed was organization, a far-seeing patriotism, the skill to temporise and establish an accord in the jarring elements of strife, and a determination to turn them to account not for private purposes of self-aggrandisement, but for carrying out into effect the traditions which the great Shiváji had fifty years ago left behind as a legacy to his people. Among the men who came to the front at this time Báláji Vishwanáth soon asserted for himself by common consent a position which pointed him out as a man who combined in himself the virtues of which the country then most stood in need. He had been a Kárkun in Dhanáji Jádhav's service, having been introduced there by a fellow Kárkun in the same service named Ábáji Purandaré, the founder of the Purandaré family. They were Dhanáji Jádhav's chief civil advisers, one a Konkanastha and the other a Déshastha Bráhman. The Deccani Bráhmans had from the first taken an important part in organizing the dominions and power of Shiváji, and many of them—the Hanmantés, the Pinglés, Ábáji Sondév, Pralhád Niráji and others had shown great abilities in the field. The Bráhmans of the Konkan had not taken any prominent part in the first sixty years of the development of the Maráthá power, but the larger opportunities now opened out to talent and ambition attracted some of their best men to try their fortunes in serving their country, and among the men who thus left their homes in the Konkan were Báláji Vishwanáth and his friend, the founder of the Bhánu family, who had been driven by the oppression of the Siddis of Janjirá. Báláji Vishwanáth and Ábáji Purandaré accompanied their master Dhanáji Jádhav when he was sent by Tárábái to oppose Sháhu's return into the Deccan. Before his death Dhanáji recommended both his trusted advisers to the notice of his new master, and Báláji made himself especially serviceable as adviser to Sháhu, so that before long, he became the chief minister in power, though not in name, and later on, when the old Péshwá Bahiropant Pinglé failed to give satisfaction to his master, Báláji was raised to his place as the Péshwá. This was the man who might be said to have, by his genius and patriotism, accomplished the task which otherwise threatened to prove almost impossible. Báláji Vishwanáth first directed all his attention to the restoration of public order, and put an end to the lawlessness which the predatory marauders of the time practised to an extent unknown before, and which made them the terror of the country. The Khatáo Bráhman freebooter was first defeated by Parashurám Trimbak's son, Sháhu's new Pratinidhi. Shankráji the old Sachiv who was in Tárábái's interest happened to die at this time; and the minor Sachiv's mother who managed his affairs was induced to join the new forces, which Báláji Vishwanáth was organizing for the defence of the country. The Thorát freebooter was attacked by Báláji Vishwanáth himself, but unfortunately for him, Báláji was captured through treachery and had to be ransomed by his master. The forces of Sachiv were sent against Thorát, but were defeated. Ultimately, however, Báláji succeeded in defeating the outlaw, and his fort was razed to the ground. The Chaván leader was temporised with by certain concessions. Negotiations were opened with Kánhoji Ángré by the old Péshwá Bahiropant; but they ended in failure, and Báláji was deputed to bring these negotiations to a successful close. By appealing to his patriotism, Ángré was prevailed upon to give up Tárábái's cause. Just about this time, the Rájá of Kolhápur also died, and a minor Rájá the son of Rájárám's younger wife, was installed in his place. This change was not brought about without a revolution in which Tárábái was displaced from power and kept in prison by Rámchandrapant, the old Pant Amátya. In all these several ways Sháhu found that the advice of his ministers had greatly improved the desperate condition of his affairs since Báláji Viswanáth and his coadjutors had joined his service.

After the minor troubles had been thus disposed of, Báláji turned his attention to establish better relations between his master Sháhu and the great Maráthá chiefs. They were too powerful to be brought under control by war or stratagem. Proposals accordingly were made to them in which they were appealed to on the higher side of their nature. Their common interests were shown to be the interests of the entire confederacy. If they stood together they were great and powerful, but if they insisted on standing apart from their fellows, the danger of isolation was pointed out to them, and it was creditable to the patriotism of these leaders that such an appeal produced its desired effect. The Chandrasén Jádhavráo and the Nimbálkar had indeed cut themselves off from the confederacy by joining with the Moghuls, but Khandéráo Dábhádé, Udájiráo Powár, Parsoji Bhonslé, and the other leaders who had thrown in their lot in the support of Sháhu's power, were appealed to with success, and arrangements were made by which not only they but the Pant Sachiv and the Pant Pratinidhi, who were the chief members of the old Ashtapradhán Councils, were similarly satisfied that their interests lay in common union. The title of Sénápati was about this time conferred on Khandéráo Dábhádé in acknowledgment of the great services he had rendered during the war and in the early years of Sháhu's rule. Similar distinctions were conferred on Parsoji Bhonslé, who was made *Séná Sáhéb Subhá*. The footing these leaders had secured for themselves in Khándésh and Bérárs was freely conceded to them, and a legitimate opening was ensured for their future successes westwards into Gujarát and eastwards in the Gondawan country. Udáji Powár's ambition was allowed a similar outlet in Málwá. These three great leaders were promised, if they co-operated with the central authority, and joined their forces together, that the sanction of the Delhi emperors would soon be obtained to give legitimacy to their pretensions. Fattésing Bhonslé of Akkalkot was also appointed to command Sháhu's army in advancing the conquest of the Karnátik in the south. The Pratinidhis, who both father and son had rendered such excellent service, the first during the war, and the second in the struggles with Kolhápur, the Khatáo Mahárája and the Siddis in the Konkan were honoured by being placed in charge of the Rájá's old dominions between the Wárná and the Nirá. Kánhoji Ángré was made the chief admiral in the service of the Maráthá power, and confirmed in his possession of the forts in the Konkan. Govindráo Chitnis, who had rendered service during the war, was similarly honoured by a military command. In this manner, power and privilege were thus distributed amongst the great leaders, while Báláji Vishwanáth contented himself with continuing to be Sháhu's principal civil adviser, his only military command being confined to certain of the Rájá's claims in distant Khándésh and Bálaghát which brought him neither power nor resources. This notable self-denial was characteristic of the man, and to a large extent it helped him in carrying out the policy which he had in view of establishing a bond of union between the great leaders whom he wished to organize for purposes of common defence and aggression. As a result of these patriotic endeavours, Báláji succeeded within ten years from the time of his joining his master's service, to give a coherent unity to the nation, and remove the causes of disunion which once threatened to break up the Maráthá power. It was no wonder therefore that the Moghul commanders and the great Vazirs at Delhi who were fighting for their own ends, soon began to show to Rájá Sháhu the respect which was felt for the traditions of Shiváji and his commanders, and before long every dissatisfied Delhi faction sought to obtain Sháhu's help in furtherance of its own interests.

This enlargement of the sphere of Maráthá influence brought on in its train a considerable modification of the civil constitution laid down by Shiváji when he ascended the throne. The leading features of this old Ashtapradhán or Council arrangements have been described in a former chapter. Sambháji's misrule and the subsequent conquest of the Deccan by Aurangzéb practically set aside this constitution. Rájárám indeed tried to build it up in his court at Gingi, but in the troublous times of the war, such a constitution could not be expected to work on its old lines. The necessities of the times required that power should be placed in strong hands, whether civil or military, and this had to be done at any cost. Pralhád Niráji virtually ruled the councils of the Maráthá forces during the eventful years of the great seige at Gingi, and on his death, Rájárám, when he returned to the Deccan, was so heavily weighted with the cares of the war that the Ashtapradhán Council was virtually in abeyance when the war was brought to an end. When Sháhu was seated on his throne at Sátárá, an attempt was made to revive the Council of the eight great ministers, but the arrangement was not suited to the altered circumstances. The Ashtapradhán Council was no doubt set up by Shiváji with great foresight, but it presupposed a well ordered centralized government. In the absence of such a government, it could not be expected to work in accord with its old traditions, and Sháhu had not the virtues of his grandfather, and did not inspire that confidence which was felt by all classes in the arrangements made by Shiváji. Moreover, the Council might work well for a small kingdom confined within narrow limits, but when, in consequence of the war, the Maráthás spread over the whole country, from the Narmadá to the Kávéri, and the leaders were holding possessions in detached places surrounded by the entire power of the Moghuls, these conditions for success were greatly wanting, and the Ashtapradhán arrangement naturally broke down. Báláji Vishwanáth saw this instinctively, and he adapted himself to the altered circumstances of the time. The Councillors still retained their dignities in Sháhu's Court at Sátárá, but real power and control did not remain in their hands except only in name, when they had to regulate Dábhádé's armies in Khándésh and Bhonslé's conquests in Bérár, and to fight with the Moghul Governors on the east and the south beyond the limits of the Maráthá territory proper. The separatist elements were always powerful in the Maráthá country, and the war and its consequences had strengthened those elements and weakened the virtues which ensured the success of central rule. Báláji Vishwanáth perceived soon that the only arrangement possible was the formation of a confederacy of the great leaders held together by the traditions of Shiváji for purposes of common action against foreign powers, but in other respects, a confederacy of co-ordinate and equal authorities in respect of internal management and control. In this way and this way only was it possible to hold together the great leaders who had established themselves by their own resources in the different parts of the country beyond their natural and territorial limits. The Maráthá territory proper was surrounded on all sides by the Moghul Governors at Sávanur, at Hyderábád, in Gujarát and Málwá, and by the Siddis, the Portuguese and the English on the west coast. These could only be held at bay by confederating the scattered Maráthá camps and in these camps by localizing power in the hands of capable men. In respect of common purposes for which all felt interested, they might and did join together and present a solidarity of interest only on condition that they were allowed to exercise internal authority within their own limits, and as long as they were animated by the old traditions, there was general safety in this union. Báláji Vishwanáth and his advisers accepted this situation, and the old Ashtapradhán arrangement gave way to the idea of a Maráthá confederacy which, for the next hundred years, was the great controller of events throughout India.

That the plan succeeded remarkably well is evidenced by the fact that it achieved not only its immediate end, but that it worked well under very trying circumstances for a hundred years and more. It enabled the Maráthás to conquer Gujarát, Málwá, Bundélkhand, Orissá, Gondawan, Némád and Karnátik down to the Tungabhadrá. It helped them to control all the states in Rajaputáná and the court at Delhi, and seat and unseat emperors there according as it suited the interests of the nation. It even carried them to the banks of the Indus on one side and to control the Nabobs of Oudh and Bengal, and Orissá on the East, and to set back the limits of the territories occupied by the Nizám at Hyderábád and the Nabob at Sávanur and the Karnátik, and later on of Hyder and Tipu. It even helped them to drive the Portuguese from Bassein and to wage two wars on equal terms with the English. It enabled the Maráthás to stand the crushing defeat at Pánipat and again to set up their rule at Delhi and over Northern India, and if after a hundred years' trial it failed, the failure was due to the fact that the traditions which guided the councils of the confederate powers in their best period gave way to other views in which the confederate idea was abandoned for purposes of individual advancement. The vitality of the confederacy was shown in the successes attained in the wars and conquests that took place during these hundred years, and it is clear that the old Asthapradhán arrangement would never have succeeded in securing this remarkable development.

Of course, there was in this strength a source of weakness also; and none was aware of the weakness better than Báláji Vishwanáth and his advisers, and their descendants. The confederacy was a rope of sand, if it was not held together by a common tradition and a common patriotism. Báláji Vishwanáth's great merit consists in the fact that while he accepted the situation, he was not oblivious to its defects. As the Ashtapradhán council could not be revived, he tried to substitute in its place other bonds of union which might minimise the defects of the inevitable change. The leading features of the new policy may be thus shortly summed up: (1) The confederacy was held together first by the traditions of Shiváji and by the reverence attached to the person of his grandson Sháhu. During the forty years' period that Sháhu was at the head of power, he continued to be regarded by every leader with affection and regard. Báláji Vishwanáth did his best to strengthen this tie which held the members of the Confederacy together. Every *sanad* granted to the civil and the military commanders had to be issued in Sháhu's name, and by his orders all titles and dignities were bestowed on them. He coined the money. Every treaty had to be made in his name, and every expedition had to be reported to him. (2) Next to this central position of Sháhu, the other great element which held together the Confederates was the sense of a balance of power kept up among the different members of the Confederacy by a judicious exercise of Sháhu's intermediation. In Báláji Vishwanáth's time the Péshwá only represented a very small military command, though he was Sháhu's chief adviser in all executive matters. When in the time of the next two Péshwás, attempts were made to increase their military power at the expense of the other commanders, Sháhu's intervention prevented this disturbance of power between the Péshwá on one side, and the Dábhádé and Gáikwád on the west coast and the Bhonslé of Nágpur, in the wars in Bengal and the Gangetic valley. Similar efforts were put forth to retain this balance of power when it was threatened later on by the great Shindiá and Holkar families, when they quarrelled among themselves or had differences with the Péshwás, the Gáikwáds and the Bhonslés. The Dábhádés and their successors the Gáikwáds, the Péshwás themselves and their great lieutenants, the Shindiás and Holkars, and later on, the Bundélés, Vinchurkars and Patwardhans,—these worked together for a hundred years under an assurance which was seldom disappointed, that the several powers would respect each others' right, and prevent their total ruin by the aggrandisement of any one of their body. This idea of mutual co-operation and of respect for each other's position constitutes the main interest of the story of the Maráthá Confederacy during these one hundred years. The equality of the several powers was guaranteed by *sanads* and treaties, and in the famous treaty made with the emperors of Delhi in Báláji Bájiráo's time, this equality was asserted by the two great lieutenants of the Péshwá standing surety for their master's fidelity to the trust accepted by him on pain of their leaving the Péshwá's cause if he broke his word. The essential idea therefore of the confederacy was that the several members thereof should enforce the preservation of a balance of power in the interests of all. It was this assurance that kept the confederacy together for so many generations. (3) Besides the two bonds of union mentioned above which held the confederacy together by sentiment and patriotism, Báláji Vishwanáth adopted the precaution of still firmly binding the different powers by making their material interests centre in the common discharge of their duties. When by the success of his diplomacy at Delhi he secured the emperor's sanction to the levying of *chouth* and *sardéshmukhi* in the Deccan, it was arranged that this work of collecting the *Bábtis* should be distributed among the two chief Ashta-pradhán members of Sháhu's Council and himself in such a way as to prevent all chance of internal conflict. The Pratinidhi, the Péshwá and the Pant Sachiv were made the collectors of the Rájá's *Bábtis* in different proportions, and in places apart from their chief possessions. This same principle was enforced, at least in theory, when *chouth* and *sardéshmukhi* levies were made beyond the limits of the Deccan *subhás*. The division of power was so arranged as to make the interests of all a common concern. (4) The great commanders also held their *inám* and *vatan* lands in the Maráthá country proper, and their fidelity was thus secured by their attachment to these hereditary possessions held by them at a distance from their camps. (5) Besides these material interests, a general obligation was placed upon all commanders to present the final accounts of their administrations into the State Treasury. A great central Fadnis or Secretariat Department was organized, where the accounts had to be examined and checked. (6) Besides the Central Treasury and the Accounts Department, each commander, large and small, of Maráthá armies and forts was accompanied by officials appointed by the Central Authority, and these officials acted as the audit officers of these commanders and were accountable to the Central Authorities when the accounts were sent up to be finally checked. The Central Authority had thus its representatives with every chief and they were intended to be reporters-general of all irregularities and complaints to the central power. These officers were called Darakadárs, and were either Diwáns, Mujumdárs, Phadnis, in the case of the great leaders, and in the case of forts and smaller chiefs, they were called Sabnis, Chitnis, Jamidárs, and Kárkhánnis, their duties being confined to audit and account only. They alone had the right to keep accounts of the local commanders, and they could not be displaced without the consent of the Central Departmental heads.

In these six different ways Báláji Vishwanáth

did his best to minimise the defects of the new system of confederate government set up by Sháhu, and while these arrangements lasted in their original integrity, the central power was powerful enough to control the entire administration. Of course, there were seeds of dissolution and decay in the arrangement, but they were fairly held in check for nearly a century. We have the testimony of Mr. Mountstuart Elphinstone and his coadjutors that though the system was theoretically full of defects, it practically ensured peace and prosperity, and succeeded in making the Maráthá power respected and feared by all its neighbours. All these checks presupposed the sanction of recognized authority without which they could not be enforced with efficacy, and the last years of Báláji Vishwanáth's life were devoted to the accomplishment of this end, i.e., to secure the recognition by the Delhi emperors of the rights of the Maráthá confederacy to the *swarájya, chouth* and *sardéshmukhi* over the whole of the empire. This acquisition gained to the Maráthá power that legitimacy, in the absence of which it is not possible to distinguish power from force. This was the crowning work of Báláji Vishwanáth's organizing genius, and though many others contributed to its success, this achievement must always be his principal claim to be regarded as next to Shiváji, the principal founder of the Maráthá Confederacy.

CHAPTER XI.

CHOUTH AND SARDÉSHMUKHI.

IN the last Chapter an attempt was made to show how order was evolved out of confusion by the constructive genius and patient skill of the first Péshwá Báláji Vishwanáth. A great deal of what is to follow had to be anticipated in that statement with a view to bring out into prominence the great transformation that took place, when the small kingdom over which Shiváji ruled was enlarged into a confederacy of states, with a common tradition and a common purpose. Báláji Vishwanáth, before his death in 1720, achieved the still greater success of securing a legitimate sanction to the larger claims put forth by the Maráthá leaders in consequence of the change that took place on Sháhu's accession to power. The story of this transference of power from the old Mahomedan rulers to the hands of the Maráthá Confederacy presents features, the like of which were seldom witnessed in the past history of India, and resembles faithfully the history of the success achieved by the great Marquis of Wellesley in the early years of this century, when he organized the system of the subsidiary alliances, as they were called, with the native powers, which secured to the British Company its sovereignty over the continent of India. This idea of the subsidiary alliances was, in fact, a reproduction on a more organized scale of the plan followed by the Maráthá leaders a hundred years in advance, when they secured the grant of the *chouth* and *sardéshmukhi* from the Imperial authorities at Delhi. The true nature of these claims to *chouth* and *sardéshmukhi*, which were conceded by the Moghul Emperor in 1719, cannot be properly understood without a brief historical review of these demands as they were first formulated by the founder of the Maráthá power fifty years before at the very commencement of his career. The first mention of these demands occurs so far back as the year 1650, when Shiváji's territory did not extend beyond the limits of his father's *jahágir* in Pooná and Supá, and a few forts near about. It seems to have been Shiváji's ambition to acquire *sardéshmukhi vatan* in the Maráthá country. His family had been respectable and even powerful for two generations, but neither his grandfather nor father could claim equality with the ancient Déshmukh families with some of whom they had formed marriage alliances such as the Ghádgés of Málawdi, the Nimbálkars of Phaltan, the Daphalés of Jat, and the Bhonslés of Sáwantwádi. These Déshmukhs claimed to have acquired their ancestral *vatans* from times coeval with the establishment of the Adilsháhi and the Nizámsháhi kingdoms. As Déshmukhs, they were responsible for the tranquillity and peace of the country, and the collection of the revenues entrusted to their charge. They used to receive about 10 per cent. of these revenues, 5 per cent. in cash or grain, and 5 per cent. in grants of arable land. Shiváji was naturally anxious to secure a grant of this *sardéshmukhi vatan,* and in 1650 he first submitted to the Emperor Shahájahán a request for the *sardéshmukhi* dues in the *Pránts* of Junnar and Ahmednagar, over which he claimed his family had hereditary *vatan* rights. Shiváji offered to enter the Moghul service with 5,000 horse if his services were accepted. Shahájahán put off this request for the time till Shiváji could submit his proposal in person at Delhi. In 1657, when Aurangzéb was in command in the Deccan under his father, Shiváji again repeated his offer. This time it was proposed that Aurangzéb should obtain the permission of his father to allow Shiváji to raise a force and seize Dábhol and other sea-coast dependencies, and protect the Deccan during Aurangzéb's absence in his wars with his rival brothers. One Raghunáthpant and Krishnáji were sent as ambassadors to Aurangzéb, and they were instructed to repeat the request for the *sardéshmukhi* grant. Aurangzéb gave the authority which Shiváji desired for the conquest of the Konkan, and as regards the *sardéshmukhi* grant, he promised to discuss the question with Shiváji's trusted adviser Ábáji Sondév, when the latter came to Delhi.

The third occasion when we find any reference made to these claims was in connection with the negotiations made between Shiváji and Rájá Jayasing at the Purandar convention in 1666, when Shiváji agreed to surrender his forts and proceed to Delhi to make his formal submission to the Emperor. In this convention Shiváji requested that an assignment should be made to him from the territories conquered from the Nizámsháhi kings and transferred to Bijápur in consideration of his hereditary claims on the Nizámsháhi government. For the first time we find in this convention a demand made not only for *sardéshmukhi*, but also for *chouth*, *i.e.* 25 per cent. of the revenue of certain Districts, the charge of collecting which *chouth*, as also 10 per cent. *sardéshmukhi*, he undertook to bear himself. In consideration of these concessions, he offered to pay peshcush to the Moghul Emperor of forty lakhs of rupees, by instalments of three lakhs yearly, and agreed further to maintain a body of troops at his own cost for the Imperial Service. Aurangzéb made no direct reply to the request about *chouth* and *sardéshmukhi*, but promised favourable consideration of the pro posals submitted by Jayasing when the latter sent the convention agreement for sanction, provided that Shiváji came to Delhi and paid peshcush. Nothing came of the visit to Delhi, and Shiváji's hopes were disappointed when the Emperor kept him a prisoner. When Shiváji later on made his escape, and commenced the war again, Aurangzéb appears to have relented, and towards 1667, he gave Shiváji a *jahágir* in Bérár with the title of a Rájá, and a *mansab* to his son Sambháji. These concessions were apparently intended to satisfy Shiváji's old claims to *chouth* and *sardéshmukhi*. Shiváji, however, was not satisfied with the concessions made, and began to insist on his own terms, and levied *chouth* and *sardéshmukhi* from the rulers of Bijápur and Golcondá. In 1668, the Bijápur Adilsháhi kings agreed to pay three lakhs of rupees on account of *chouth* and *sardéshmukhi*, and the Golcondá ruler agreed to pay five lakhs about the same time. In 1671, *chouth* and *sardéshmukhi* levies were recovered from the Moghul province of Khándésh. In 1674, the Portuguese possessions in the Konkan were made to pay tribute by way of *chouth* and *sardéshmukhi* for that part of the country. In return for the tributes paid by the Bijápur and Golcondá rulers, Shiváji undertook to protect them from the aggressions of the Moghuls, and this protection was found very effective in the wars which took place about that time. The Rájá of Bédnore and the Chief of Soondá also agreed to pay tribute to Shiváji, and in 1676, when Shiváji invaded the Karnátik, *chouth* and *sardéshmukhi* demands were enforced in those distant possessions. Before his death in 1680, Shiváji had thus established his system of subsidiary and tributary alliances with the consent of the Mahomedan and Hindu rulers in Southern India whom he protected, and he enforced his demands on some of the Moghul provinces also. The *sardéshmukhi* claim was in its origin, a request for hereditary *vatan*, burdened with the charge of revenue collections. The demand for *chouth* was subsequently added with the consent of the powers whose protection was undertaken against foreign aggression, on payment of fixed sums for the support of the troops maintained for such service. This was the original idea as worked out by Shiváji, and it was this same idea which in the Marquis of Wellesley's hand bore such fruit a hundred and twenty-five years later.

When the War of Independence was over, and the Maráthá leaders had established themselves in the Karnátik, Gangathadi, Bérárs, Khándésh, and the frontiers of Gujarát and Málwá, this idea naturally received an expansion, and in the negotiations which took place with the Moghul Governors, Báláji Vishvanáth and the other advisers of Sháhu found it necessary to introduce considerable modifications. While the war was still going on, there was no room for negotiations about *chouth* and *sardéshmukhi*, and even when it was ended, the first object of the leaders was to secure the restoration of the *Swarájya*, *i.e.*, to restore to Sháhu the territories held by his grandfather when he was crowned King at Ráigad in 1674. After Rájárám's death, Aurangzéb appears to have made the first advance by recognizing Sháhu's rights to a portion of the *swarájya.* He assigned to Sháhu as a marriage dowry his old *jahágir* at Supá and Indápur, as also the *mahâls* of Akkalkot and Névásá. Later on, Aurangzéb induced Sháhu to send letters to the Maráthá Commanders desiring them to stop the war and submit to the Emperor. The use made of Sháhu's agency for this purpose was a distinct recognition of his claim to be the leader of the Maráthá forces which were then fighting with the Moghuls. In 1705, with a view to bring this war to an end, Aurangzéb was prevailed upon to consent to the payment of 10 per cent. of the whole revenue of the six *subhás* of the Deccan as *sardéshmukhi*, for which the Maráthá Commanders were to agree to maintain order with a body of horse. This was the first formal recognition by Aurangzéb of the claims which Shiváji had put forth nearly fifty years previously for the *sardéshmukhi* grant. Nothing came of this proposal as the Maráthá leaders raised their terms, and the war was continued to the end. On Aurangzéb's death, owing to their internecine quarrels, his sons found it necessary to bring the war to a close, and Sháhu was released and was allowed to proceed to his country, and he was informed that if he succeeded in establishing his power in the Deccan, Zulfikarkhán, the Moghul Commander, and his master Azimsháh, the Emperor's son, would restore to him the territories conquered by Shiváji with additional *jahágirs* between the Bhimá and the Godávari. When Sháhu established himself at Sátárá, the Moghul Governor of the Deccan, Dawood Khán, for the first time entered into a formal alliance with the Maráthá leaders conceding to them the *chouth* or 25 per cent of the revenues of certain provinces, and the *chouth* was to be collected by Sháhu's own agents. This arrangement lasted for four years from 1709 to 1713, when Dawood Khán was removed and Nizám-ul-mulk was appointed *subhédár*. The Nizám refused to carry out the arrangement made by Dawood Khán and the war commenced, and went on till 1715, when peace was concluded and Sháhu was appointed to the command of 10,000 horse in the Moghul service. Nizám-ul-mulk was recalled from the Deccan, and one of the Sayyads was appointed Governor in his place by the new Emperor. This Sayyad Subhédár, to strengthen his own position, engaged the services of an old Maráthá veteran Bráhman named Shankráji who had served in the war at Gingi and had since retired to Benáres. He was sent as an ambassador to Sháhu, and between Shankráji on one side and Báláji Vishvanáth on the other, arrangements were made for the restoration of the *swarájya* and the grant of the *chouth* and *sardéshmukhi* of the six

Deccan *subhás.* The old Karnátik *jahágir* was also to be restored, and the Nágpurkar Bhonslé's conquests in Bérár were to be confirmed. On his side Sháhu agreed to pay Peshkash of ten lakhs of rupees to the Emperor, and to preserve peace against depredations from all quarters and keep a body of 15,000 horse in the Emperor's service to be placed at the disposal of the Governors, *fouzdárs,* and other officers in charge of the Deccan districts. These terms proposed by Báláji Vishvanáth on behalf of his master were communicated through Shankráji to the Sayyad who agreed to the terms as proposed, and a draft treaty was drawn up. The Sayyad stipulated that the territories not in his possession in Southern India, Mysore, Trichinopoly and Tanjore, might be recovered by Sháhu with his own resources and at his own cost. Sháhu at once sent 10,000 horse to serve as contingent with the Sayyad's army, and all the Maráthá commanders of note accompanied this force, the chief being Santáji Bhonslé, a relation of the *Séná Sáhéb Subhá,* Udáji Powár, and Vishwásráo Áthawlé. The terms agreed to by the Sayyad were submitted for the sanction of the Emperor, but the sanction was refused, as the Emperor was not disposed to follow the advice of the Sayyad. The latter thereupon marched to Delhi. A strong Maráthá force of 15,000 troops accompanied the Sayyad, and Khandéráo Dábhádé, Báláji Vishvanáth, Mahádáji Bhánu and others accompanied this force. After a slight opposition, in which Santáji Bhonslé and Mahádáji Bhánu were killed in a street tumult, the Emperor was put to death, and his successor Mahomed Sháh gave the three *sanads* for the *swarájya*, *chouth*, and *sardéshmukhi*, to Báláji Vishwanáth on behalf of his master Sháhu Mahárái.

Thus after a continuous struggle for seventy years, the objects which Shiváji had formulated when he first put forth his claims in 1650, were successfully accomplished by the leaders who guided the counsels of Sháhu. Not only was the old *swarájya* restored, but its limits were extended so as to embrace all the conquests then made, and an opening was made for possible extensions in the future. The *swarájya sanad* included the country above the Gháts, Shiváji's old conquests between the Hiranyakéshi river in the South and the Indráyani on the North being the Western Mávals of Pooná, Sátárá and Kolhápur. These territories were Pooná, Supá, Bárámati, Mával, Indápur, Junner, Wái, Sátárá, Karhád, Khatáo, Mánd, Phaltan, Taralá, Malkápur, Azrè, Panhálá and Kolhápur. Towards the East, the greatest extension was along the valley of the Bhimá and Nirá rivers. Below the Gháts the *swarájya* included the Northern and Southern Konkans, Rámnagar, Javár, Chaul, Bhivadi, Kalyán, Rájápur, Dábhol, Rájápuri, Fondá, and a portion of North Kanará, Akolá and Kudál. In the extreme South, Gadag, Halyál, Béllráry, and Kopal were held by Shivájí to keep up his communications with Tanjore and Gingi. On the North-east side, Shivájí's possessions included detached posts in Sangamnér, Bág-lan, Khándésh and Bérár. This narrow and irregular strip which constituted the *swa-rájya* was restored to Sháhu, excepting Khándésh, in exchange for which an extension was allowed on the Pandharpur side of the Bhimá valley. The six subhás over which the right of levying *chouth* was conceded, included Bérár, Khándésh, Auran-gábád, Bédar, Hyderábád and Bijápur. In the accounts of the Empire the six subhás were supposed to yield in all eighteen crores of rupees on which the *sardéshmukhi* charge represented one-tenth, and the *chouth* would be one-fourth. The necessity of such a re-cognition of these rights by the Emperor had forced itself upon Báláji Vishvanáth's mind by the fact that no other measure would have restored tranquillity to the country. There was no permanence in the arrangements by which the different commanders had established their power in different parts of the Deccan. Each great leader was fully alive to the fact that it was their common interest to establish a bond of union between the old and the new order of things, between the Moghul Governors and *fouzdárs* and civil rulers of all kinds, and the Maráthá Commanders who established themselves in power on these old foundations. The *sanad* for the *chouth* stipulated that Sháhu should retain 15,000 horse in the Emperor's service. They were to be kept in the different districts at the disposal of the Moghul governors. The *chouth* was, unlike the *sardéshmukhi*, not a *vatan*, but a payment for service in the shape of protecting the country and preventing foreign aggression. If all the six subhás had been brought under contribution at the figure mentioned in the *sanad*, they would have yielded four crores and a half of rupees, but the country had been so devastated by Aurangzéb's wars and conquests, that the actual yield was not one-fourth that amount. The proportion of 25 per cent. for the *chouth* levie was apparently fixed upon the understanding that the local expenses of Government under the Moghul empire were about one-fourth of the entire collections. This *chouth* collection was undertaken by the Maráthá leaders and was conceded to them because it involved no real loss of the net revenue which reached the hands of the central authorities at Delhi, being 75 per cent. of the total collections. Owing, however, to the depressed state of the country, the *sardéshmukhi* and *chouth* revenue nearly absorbed the whole of the actual receipts, and left but little that could reach the Imperial exchequer. This source of irritation remained notwithstanding the grant of the *sanads*. The Rájá's *bábtis* as they were called, 10 per cent. for *sardéshmukhi*, and 25 per cent. for *chouth*, were rigidly enforced wherever the Maráthá arms were strong enough to prevail. The remaining three-fourths of the estimated collections were left to the old Governors, who were, however, unable to enforce their recovery, and gradually power fell into the hands of the Maráthá leaders.

This transfer of power did not take place without a struggle. The Emperor could grant the *sanads*, but it was not so easy to require the Governors to give effect to their master's wishes. The Nizám-ul-Mulk, who was the Subhédár of the Deccan after the fall of the Sayyads, was steadily opposed to the concession his master had made under pressure, and for the next twenty years the Maráthá leaders were engaged in an uninterrupted contest with the Nizám, in which Báláji Vishvanáth's son Bájiráo, the second Péshwá, chiefly distinguished himself. At first the Nizám temporized, and offered to recognize the grants made by the Emperor to Sháhu. After the fall of the Sayyads, the Nizám, professing to side with the Kolhápur Rájá, whom he took under his protection, set up his rival pretensions against the collectors sent by Sháhu's Government. Bájiráo succeeded in overcoming this opposition, and a fresh *firman* was obtained in 1722. Later on, the Nizám raised a fresh dispute questioning Sháhu's claim to the *chouth* and *sardéshmukhi* on the ground that he failed to carry out his engagement to preserve the tranquillity of the Deccan. Misunderstandings followed, and force had to be used to remove this opposition. By making convenient exchanges of territory, and conceding exemption from the *chouth* and *sardéshmukhi* demands to the territory in the immediate vicinity of Hyderábád, the Nizám was at last prevailed on to reaffirm the validity of the grants made by the Emperor. About the year 1730, fresh opposition was raised by the Nizám in concert with the

Kolhápur Rájá, who pretended to be a sharer in these *chouth* and *sardéshmukhi* dues. The Nizám, however, was again thwarted by the superior tactics of the Péshwá, and he was forced to give up the support he extended to the Rájá of Kolhápur. The Rájá was himself defeated by Sháhu's Commander, the Pratinidhi, and a final treaty of partition was made between the Sátárá and Kolhápur Rájás by which Sháhu was left sole master under his imperial grants of *chouth*, *sardéshmukhi* and *swarájya* in the six Deccan subhás, while the Kolhápur Rájá had to content himself with the possessions south of the Wárná up to the Tungabhadrá river. The imperial grants became accordingly, after three wars and two confirmations, the recognized rule of the Empire about the year 1732, and binding alike on all the contesting powers. The causes of dispute were of course not entirely removed, but the wars which subsequently took place between the succeeding Nizáms and Maráthá leaders did not involve the question of the legitimacy of the rights conferred by the Emperors. In 1743, a dispute occurred between the Maráthá leaders and the then Nizám Salábatjang. The Nizám was defeated, and all the territories in Khándésh and Násik were annexed to the dominions of the Maráthás by a treaty of peace between the two powers In 1760 another dispute arose, and Maráthá arms prevailed against the Nizám's forces, and a large accession of territories towards Ahmednagar and the Ahmednagar fort were added to the Péshwá's dominions. About 1790 similar differences arose, and portions of the Solápur and Bijápur Districts were similarly annexed to the Péshwá's dominions. In the Karnátik, the fight which the Maráthá leaders had to maintain was not with the Nizám, but with the Sávanur Nabábs, and in three successive wars with these Nabábs, which were carried on by the Péshwá Bájiráo, and his son Báláji, the districts of Bijápur, Bélgaum, and Dhárwár were successively added to the Péshwá's dominions. These Karnátik wars had to be continued further on in the century after the downfall of the Sávanur Nabábs with Hyder and his son Tipu who rose to power in Mysore from 1760 to 1790. These successive wars resulted in the defeat of the Mysore rulers, and the extension of the Maráthá dominions to the Tungabhadrá. The same success attended the wars waged with the Portuguese and the Siddis of Janjirá by Chimáji Appá, the brother of Bájiráo Péshwá, and Báláji Bájiráo the third Péshwá. In these several ways nearly the whole of the

Maháráshtra country proper thus came into the hands of the members of the Maráthá Confederacy in the course of the century. These extensions of territory were the results of conquests, but they had their origin in the rights conferred by the grants of *chouth* and *sardéshmukhi*. The word *swarájya*, in consequence of these extensions, gradually obtained a much wider expansion than was comprised in the old grant. And the right to levy the *chouth* and *sardéshmukhi*, which was at first confined to the six subhás south of the Tapti river under these *sanads*, was twenty years later confirmed and extended on the same principles, to the whole of the empire, so as to embrace the territories to the North, including Gujarát, Káthiávár, Málvá, Rajputáná Bundélkhand, the Doáb, Nimuch, Gondawana, Sambalpur, Orissá, Ágra, Delhi, Oudh and Bengal. This extension of power and influence will form the subject of a later chapter, but the essential features were the same as those which have been treated of above. The *chouth* and *sardéshmukhi* rights served, in the hands of the Maráthá leaders, the same purpose of giving legitimacy and expansion to their power which in the last century has resulted from the subsidiary alliances and conquests made by the British Government. This story of expansion derives its chief interest from the fact that the members of the confederacy achieved these conquests not as single states, so much as by acting together in concert. It contrasts significantly with the fate which overtook the policy of isolation, at Kolhápur and Tanjore, which states were cut off from the larger life which the rights conferred by the *chouth* and *sardéshmukhi* grants secured to Péshwás, Gáikwárs, Sindiás, Holkars, Bhonslés, Vinchurkars, the Patawardhans, Bundélé and other members of the Confederacy. Sháhu's Councillors, on a memorable occasion, seriously discussed the question whether the policy of expansion represented by the Péshwá Bájiráo, or the counsel of caution advised by the Pratinidhi should prevail. Fired by the eloquence of the Péshwá, Sháhu gave the weight of his support to the policy of concerted advance, and the results achieved by this confederate action of the powers are matters of history. The failure of the opposite policy of isolation, enforced partly by its position, was perhaps best illustrated in the oldest conquests of the Maráthás in Southern India, and it is proposed in the next chapter to illustrate the contrast presented by the expansion noticed above with the inglorious story of this separated branch of the Maráthá race represented by the descendants of Shiváji's brother enthroned at Tanjore.

CHAPTER XII.

MARÁTHÁS IN SOUTHERN INDIA.

NEITHER Mr. Grant Duff nor any of the native writers of Maráthi *Bakhars* have given much attention to the fortunes of the Maráthá colony in the far South at Tanjore, though the Maráthá dominion there was of an older date than in many other parts of India, and the family which ruled at Tanjore for nearly two centuries, 1675—1855, was closely allied to the founder of the Maráthá power in Western India. The chequered story of this distant and ill-fated principality confirms our view that the strength of the Maráthá power lay essentially in its union as a confederacy. Those who held themselves aloof from this union of interests and national sympathy were not allowed a place in Maráthá history proper, either by native or foreign writers. The moral of this unnatural separation has a mournful interest which enforces attention. The imporatnce of the permanent influence exercised by this distant military settlement of the Maráthás on the banks of the

"Káveri" can be best judged by a study of the census statistics of 1881, which show that the Maráthá population in the Madrás Presidency was nearly 230,000, to which we might add 20,000 more for Mysore and Cochin and Trávancore, making a total of two lakhs and a half, distributed as follows:—

(1)	Ganjam	205
(2)	Vizagapatam	364
(3)	Godávari	634
(4)	Krishná	1,414
(5)	Néllore	807
(6)	Cuddápáh	3,973
(7)	Kurnool	4,081
(8)	Béllúry	14,169
(9)	Chingalpat	1,635
(10)	North Arcot	11,662
(11)	South Arcot	1,957
(12)	Tanjore	14,421
(13)	Trichinopoly	1,766
(14)	Madurá	1,943
(15)	Tinnenelly	837
(16)	Sálem	7,906
(17)	Coimbatore	2,550
(18)	Nilgiris	730
(19)	Malabár	6,107
(20)	South Kanará	147,390
(21)	Madrás City	4,238
(22)	Padukota	660

There is thus not a district in that Presidency which has not a small Maráthá colony of settlers who have permanently made it their home. South Kanará and Malabár, Cochin and Trávancore, with a Maráthá population of one lakh and a half, were of course colonized from the coast, and these settlements had no connection with the political domination established in the middle of the seventeenth century by the army of Shaháji and his son Vénkoji, the step-brother of Shiváji. As might be expected, the city of Tanjore and the districts in its neighbourhood, North Arcot, Sálem, and Madrás City, show the largest aggregates of the foreign Maráthá settlers whose ancestors accompanied Shaháji and his son to the South. Tanjore has been very happily styled by the Mahárájá of Trávancore as the southern home of the Maráthás, and though fifty years have passed since the principality was declared to have lapsed to Government for want of heirs, the *Ránis* of the palace still live in the city in the enjoyment of state pensions and a large private estate. When the kingdom was first founded between 1666—1675, the district of Tanjore included portions of South Arcot and the whole of the Trichinopoly district. The military settlers included both Bráhmans and Maráthás, and by reason of their isolation from their distant home, the sub-divisions which separated these castes in their mother-country were forgotten, and they were all welded together under the common name of Déshasthás.

The Tanjore Rájás were all of them great patrons of learning; some of them were poets and scholars themselves of no mean repute, and their charities were on a scale which arrests attention. The Tanjore Library is the largest collection of the kind to be found in any Native Court in India. The cultivation of the fine arts, music, both vocal and instrumental, etc., was carried to perfection, and Tanjore attained in those days a pre-eminence which it still retains of being the most refined and cultured district of the Southern Presidency. After the fall of Tanjore, the professors of those arts removed to Trávancore, and gave that State the reputation it now enjoys. The great city of Kombhakonam has a large sprinkling of distinguished Maráthá families whose representatives, Sir T. Mádhavráo, Diwán Bahádur Raghunáthráo, Vénkaswámi Ráo, Gopál Ráo, etc., have risen to great distinction, each in his own line, and some

16

of them have even attained an Indian reputation for statesmanship, learning and philanthropy. The Native States of Trávancore and Mysore have afforded scope to the display of the highest abilities of some of these Maráthá statesmen, both in the last and in the present century. The services of the Trávancore Minister, English Subbaráo, are well known, and one of his successors, Sir T. Mádhavráo, rescued that State from disorder and insolvency, and turned it into a model State, and the father of Diwán Bahádur Raghunáthráo achieved equal distinction in Mysore.

In North Arcot the little *jahágir* of "*Arni*" is still in the enjoyment of a Maráthá Bráhman Chief, whose ancestors acquired it originally as a fief for military service from the Bijápur King more than two hundred years ago. There were other Maráthá Bráhmans who entered in those days the services of the Nabáb of Arcot, and rose to distinction, and were known distinctively as Nizámsháhi Bráhmans. Similarly the small State of Padukota, which still retains its subordinate integrity, has a large Maráthá population, and its affairs were administered by many Bráhman Diwáns, and the most distinguished of these belonged to the family of Maráthá settlers in the south. The Native State of Cochin contains a large Maráthá population, chiefly Bráhmans of different sects who are engaged in mercantile pursuits. In the district of Bélláry there is another small Maráthá State at Sondá which has survived the general decay of Maráthá power in the south. Its founder came of the stock of the famous Santáji Ghorpadé, whose grandson Murárráo Ghorpadé played such an important part in the Karnátik wars in the middle of the eighteenth century, and who ruled over a small kingdom at Gooty till Hyder Náik conquered that principality. When the Maráthás were hard-pressed by Aurangzéb in Mahárashtra, Rájárám the second son of Shiváji retired to Gingi, which had been held as a fort by Shaháji and it was this fort which stood the seven years' siege towards the close of the seventeenth century which allowed him and the Maráthás to rally in the struggle with Aurangazéb.

It will be seen from this brief *resumé* that a handful of Maráthás, scarcely exceeding at the best one lakh of men, not only carved out kingdoms and *jahágirs* for themselves in the troublous times which succeeded the downfall of the Mahomedan power, but that their influence has not yet spent itself, and that they even now form a most interesting section of the population of that Presidency, though it must be confessed, their predominance is now decidedly on the wane. It is on this account that the story of the conquest of Tanjore must be allowed a place in a narrative which professes to deal with the fortunes of the Maráthá people more than those of any particular section of its confederate rulers.

The first entrance of the Maráthás in Southern India took place under the leadership of Shaháji Bhonslé, the father of Shiváji, in 1638. He led an army as a general in the service of the Adilsháhi Bijápur kings. These Karnátik wars kept Shaháji, and his army engaged for thirty years, and he conquered Mysore, Véllore, and Gingi. In reward for his services, Shaháji obtained a *jahágir*, which included Bangalore, Kollar, Sera or Cuttá and other places in Mysore in 1648. In the course of these wars, Shaháji forced the old náik chiefs of Madurá and Tanjore to submit to the suzerain authority of Bijápur and pay tribute. During the varying fortunes of his long career, Shaháji continued to retain the enjoyment of his *jahágirs* in the Mysore territory down to his death in 1664. Bangalore was his headquarters, and was in those days the most southerly encampment of the Maráthá armies in the south. When his son Vénkoji succeeded to this *jahágir*, there were some internecine disputes between the náik rulers of Tanjore and Madurá, and the Tanjore prince was defeated in the struggle. He then sought refuge at the Bijápur Court, and that Court ordered Vénkoji to place the Tanjore prince on his throne. Vénkoji marched at the head of 12,000 troops and obtained a great victory, and established the refugee Prince on his throne. The adherents of the Prince, however, quarrelled among themselves, and Vénkoji was invited by one of the factions to seize the fort of Tanjore. The Tanjore Prince fled at the approach of the Maráthás. Tanjore was taken by Vénkoji in 1674, and he removed his headquarters from Bangalore to Tanjore in 1675.

The most noteworthy event during the period of Vénkoji's rule over Tanjore, was the expedition of Shiváji in those parts of the country in 1676. Shiváji obtained easy possession of the Karnátik *jahágir* of the family, and Vénkoji was unable to maintain his position. The Bijápur government recognized Shiváji's claim to the Karnátik *jahágir*, including Tanjore and Trichinopoly. Vénkoji was filled with despair at this success of his half brother, and resolved to be a *Byrági*, and retire from the world, but Shiváji wrote a characteristic letter to his brother, and reminding him of his duty, dissuaded him from becoming a *Byrági*. Shiváji at this time generously yielded all his claims to his father's patrimony to satisfy his brother. This generosity had the desired effect, and Vénkoji continued to be in charge of his principality down to the time of his death in 1687. In the interest of the Maráthá confederacy it would certainly have been better if Shiváji had strengthened his hold in these parts at this time. By his abandonment of the kingdom to Vénkoji, he cut off this settlement from its proper place in the united Maráthá kingdom, and Tanjore suffered grievously by reason of this isolation. Vénkoji was not a strong ruler, and in consequence of his inability to retain his distant possession in Mysore, he was obliged to make Bangalore over to the Mysore Rájás, who purchased this Maráthá town for the small sum of three lakhs. These cessions cut off the Tanjore kingdom completely from its parent source in the Deccan, and it was not long before it was hemmed in on one side by the English, and on the other by the Mysore rulers Hyder Ali and his son Tipu.

After Vénkoji's death in 1687, his three sons, Shaháji, Sarfoji and Tukoji, succeeded to the kingdom one after another, and their joint occupation of the throne extended over a period of nearly fifty years (1687—1735). The principal event in the reign of Shaháji was the invasion of Tanjore by the Moghul General Zulfikarkhán. After Sambháji's death, and the capture of his son Sháhu by the Moghuls, the Maráthás found it impossible to oppose Aurangzéb's power in their native country of the Deccan, and Rájárám, the second son of Shiváji, with the Maráthá generals and statesmen who still adhered to the national standard, retreated to the south, and established themselves at Gingi in the neighbourhood of Pondicherry. The Moghul invaders, thereupon, marched to the south and beseiged Gingi. The operations of the seige were protracted over many years with varied success, and it was in the course of these operations that the Moghul Commander levied contributions from Tanjore, and deprived the Rájá of a portion of his territory in the Trichinopoly district. Under the rule of the two succeeding monarchs, Sarfoji and Tukoji, the Tanjore Maráthás extended their power over the Marva country in the neighbourhood of Rámésh-var. The Zamindáris of Shiv Gangá and Rámnáth were conquered about 1730. They were fiefs which acknowledged the supremacy of Tanjore when it was governed by strong rulers, and resisted its power under weak sovereigns.

The final conquest of this part of the country was effected in 1763 and 1771, by the Maráthá generals, Sidoji and Mánkoji, who greatly distinguished themselves, and Mánkoji also played a considerable part in the war between 1742 and 1763.

After the death of the three sons of Vénkoji, there was a rapid succession of rulers between 1735 and 1740, due partly to the untimely death of some, and partly to the attempts of the Moghul Commanders to impose their own nominees as kings. The Maráthá officers in the service of Tanjore finally succeeded in raising to the throne Pratápsing, an illegitimate son of Tukoji, in 1740, and he reigned for a period of twenty-three years.

The early years of Pratápsing's reign witnessed, however, the second invasion of Southern India by the confederate army of the Sátárá Rájá led by Raghuji Bhonslé of Nágpur. It was one of the largest expeditions sent out from Sátárá, and the army would have accomplished permanent results, if the Tanjore Maráthás had forgotten their jealousies, and Raghuji had pushed on his conquests after his first successes near Trichinopoly. As it was, he was content to leave a garrison at Trichinopoly, and capture Chandásáhéb, who was brought captive to Sátárá. The Péshwás were about this time anxious to strike the axe at the root of the Moghul power in North India, and this expedition to the South was undertaken by Raghuji in pursuance of the alternative policy which found support with some of the Maráthá chiefs who advised Sháhu to leave North India to itself, and seize the southern provinces permanently. Raghuji Bhonslé, on his return from this expedition, found enough occupation in Bengal and Eastern India, and the South remained closed to Maráthá influences till the rise of Hyder Ali. The release of Chandásáhéb by Sháhu at the instance of Dupleix, the French Governor of Pondicherry led to the ten years' war between the

English and the French 1750—1760. The Tanjore Rájás sided with Mahomed Ali, the English protégé, and suffered at the hands of the French ally, Murráráo Ghorpadé, who sacked Tanjore at a time when the English were unable to help the Rájá. Later on, the French general Lally also plundered Tanjore, but the English succeeded in sending relief on this occasion. Throughout these Karnátik wars, the Tanjore army under Mánkoji played an important part on the side of the English and against the French.

Notwithstanding all these sacrifices made by the Tanjore Rájás in helping the cause of the English, the Nabáb Mahomed Ali cherished a grudge against Tanjore, which was noted for its riches, and the interposition of the English alone succeeded in 1762 in establishing an understanding by which the Rájá became a tributary of the Nabáb, with an English guarantee, and agreed to pay four lakhs as tribute. Later on, in 1771, the Nabáb secured the help of the Madras Government in attacking Tulsáji, the son of Pratápsing, and Tulsáji had to sue for peace which involved him and his State in heavy money liabilities, and curtailed still more the resources of the

Tanjore State. In this second treaty the interests of the Rájá of Tanjore were completely sacrificed to the greed of Mahomed Ali, and of his English creditors, who dictated the policy of the Madras Government. The guarantee of 1762, by which the English had undertaken to be responsible for the autonomy of Tanjore, was thrown to the winds. In 1773, further acts of spoliation were renewed by the Nabáb with the help of his English allies, and the Rájá was taken prisoner, his city was captured, and the territory was annexed by the Nabáb to his own Kingdom. All these acts of spoliation and breach of faith had been undertaken by the Madras Government on their own responsibility, and in the interests of the English creditors of the Nabáb. The Court of Directors had no knowledge of them, and when they came to know the full details of these unjust proceedings, they strongly condemned the conduct of the Madras Government. They at once recalled the Governor, and resolved upon setting up Tulsáji on his ancestral throne. These orders were accordingly carried out in 1776. During the three years of the Nabáb's rule he succeeded, however, in despoiling the country of all its resources, and it took full ten years to restore to it a part of its old prosperity. Just then a war broke out between the English and Hyder Ali, and Hyder wreaked his vengeance on the ill-fated province of Tanjore by desolating it again with his plundering hordes in 1782. It was in the midst of these accumulated troubles that Tulsáji died in 1787, after having reigned eleven years. Tanjore had cut itself adrift from its parent source, and the invasions of the Maráthás and their victories over Hyder brought no relief to Tanjore, hemmed in as it was between the English and Hyder. It suffered so grievously during these twenty years that it never rallied again, even when peace was restored to Southern India after the fall of Tipu. It also suffered from internal dissensions. Tulsáji's adopted son was displaced by his half-brother Amarsing. The money liabilities due to the Madras Government had so increased by this time, and the resources of the State had been so greatly reduced, that the Rájá was unable to meet his engagements. Sarfoji, the adopted son of Tulsáji, found a protector and friend in Mr. Schwartz, the Danish missionary, and the Court of Directors recognized his claim to succeed, and he was placed in 1798 on the throne, and Amarsing was forced to retire on pension. The Marquis of

Wellesley, when he settled Mysore after the fall of Tipu, succeeded also in inducing Sarfoji to part with all exercise of power over his State, and become a titular Rájá on a fixed pension made payable to him out of the revenues. He lived on the enjoyment of this dignity and pension till his death in 1833, and was succeeded by his son who died in 1845 without any male heir. The Tanjore State was then declared to have lapsed to the Company, and the Ránees were pensioned and allowed to occupy their old palace. Their private property had also been taken away from them, but this was restored to them after many years of unsuccessful litigation.

This, in short, is the unfortunate story of this little military settlement of the Maráthás in the far South. While the confederate Maráthás were able to hold their own against the power of the Moghuls, and to recover their independence after a struggle carried on for twenty years, this little settlement, by refusing to be a member of the confederacy, and trying to shift for itself, was engulfed in the wars of the Karnátik. It virtually ceased to be a leading indepedent State in 1762. There can be no doubt that if it had kept up its connection with the parent State, it would have played a most useful part in the several invasions of the Maráthás, which took place between 1762 and 1792, and in all which the Maráthá arms prevailed, and both Hyder and Tipu had to purchase peace by agreeing to pay heavy subsidies and cession of territories. Tanjore suffered the same fate as the other Maráthá settlement at Gooty, and for the same fault, namely, that it cut itself off from the confederacy, and tried to shift for itself. This is the lesson which the story of this little settlement is well calculated to teach ; and it is a lesson which illustrates the strength and the weakness of the Maráthá power—strong when confederate, and unable to retain independence when the union was broken up.

CHAPTER XIII.

APPENDIX.

GLEANINGS FROM MARÁTHÁ CHRONICLES.

IT is well-known, that the standard (1) history of the Maráthás by Captain James Grant Duff is based, to a considerable extent, on Maráthá Bakhars or chronicles and other original papers and documents, to which the author had access. Of several of these, Grant Duff had copies made, which, he tells us (2) in his history, were deposited by him with the Literary Society of Bombay. This was certainly the most appropriate thing to do at that time, so as to provide facilities for students of Maráthá History to examine for themselves the original materials which Grant Duff had worked up into his book. Unfortunately, however, the Literary Society has long ceased to exist. And Grant Duff's Manuscripts cannot now be traced anywhere. I have had inquiries and search made in the library of the Bombay Branch of the Royal Asiatic Society, which

(1) See *inter alia* Journal Bombay Branch, Royal Asiatic Society, Vol. IX. pp. VI, IX, XXXIII and Vol. X., p. 120.

(2) See the foot notes to his History *passim*.

is the successor of the Literary Society. But the Manuscripts are not in that library and nothing on the records of either Society now available affords any clue to their present whereabouts. An impression has existed for several years past in some quarters, (3) that the Manuscripts in question were burnt, with the knowledge, if not under the orders, of Grant Duff himself. I have never, however, been able to ascertain the basis on which this impression is founded. (4) And the story itself is so improbable, and so much like the stories about the

---

(3) See *inter alia* Vividhajnânsvistâra, Vol. VIII, p. 213, Vol. IX, p. 247. A review of Grant Duff's History of the Maráthás by a student of the Poona College (now Ráo Bahádur Nilkanth Janárdan Kirtané,) p. 9 *et seq.* .

I am told that no such impression has existed at Sátárá where Grant Duff was officially employed.

(4) The basis alleged in the Review mentioned in note (2) is certainly very unsubstantial, and not to be implicitly relied on, under the circumstances. A certain "Southern Commissioner" is also mentioned as having had some share in the destruction of the Mss. The name of the gentleman who gave the information on which this story is based is mentioned in the second edition of the Review, p. 28. But I do not see that that improves matters very much. Mr. Kirtané himself has in his second edition (p. 95-7) very properly and candidly expressed his disbelief in the story, together with the grounds for his disbelief. It is, perhaps, worthy of note in this connexion, that it appears from Sir H. Elliott's History of India, by Prof. Dowson, Vol. VII, pp. vi and 210, that another of Grant Duff's Mss.—a translation of a Musalman original—is also not now forthcoming.

burning of papers and documents by the Inám Commission, that it does not deserve any further consideration. It must have originally arisen probably when it was ascertained that the Manuscripts were not on the shelves of the Library of the Bombay Branch of the Royal Asiatic Society.

Some of these documents, however, have within the last ten or twelve years become accessible to the Maráthi reader in print. And with these, there have also been published some others, which apparently were not before Grant Duff. An examination of both these groups of documents discloses sundry passages of interest in connection with Maráthá History, although it did not fall within the scope of Grant Duff's work to cast any except a very incidental and hurried glance at them, and that, too, only at some of them. Grant Duff's work devotes itself mainly, if one may not even say exclusively, to the purely political history of the Maráthás. Their social and religious progress receives only a very occasional and very indirect notice in its pages. It is true, that even in the original documents above alluded to, the various political transactions of the periods to which they respectively relate form almost exclusively the subject-matter of the narrative. (5) Still, when these original documents are before us, the incidental references contained in them to social and religious matters are even now capable of being utilized, while in the case of the Manuscripts that are lost, this is necessarily not the case. And for the reasons stated, we cannot now have access even at second-hand to such references as may have been contained in them. Considering that taken altogether, the light thrown on the socia and religious history of the Maráthás by the documents now available is not very plentiful, but comes, so to say, in only scattered rays, it is a subject of just regret, that even the chance of adding to it an extra ray here and there is now foreclosed by the loss of Grant Duff's Manuscripts. In default of them, however, it is proposed in the present paper, to gather together to a focus such of these scattered rays as may be obtained from the papers and documents which have, within the last few years, been made generally acccessible in print, in the pages of the *Vividhajnánavistára*, of the

(5) In Sir H. Elliot's History of India by Prof. Dowson, Vol. I, pp. XIX—XXI, one may read some very bitter, but not, I fear, unfounded complaints, about the character of the chronicles written by Hindu writers which Sir H. Elliott had to examine.

Kâyastha Prabhûnchyâ Itihâsâchin Sâdhanên, and above all in those of the *Kâvyêtihâsa Sangraha*. (6)

The first point of interest, then, to be noted here is the attitude of the State towards the social and religious concerns of the people. Here we are enabled to go back to the very beginnings of Maráthá power, to the system established by its great founder. And it is to be remarked, that in spite of the unfavourable conditions then existing, in spite of the all-engrossing militarism of the day, (7) Shiváji found time to apply his genius to the elaboration of a regular system of Civil Administration (8), in a manner to which we find almost no parallel throughout the whole period of

(6) These are the principal sources. Some others have also been utilised, as will be seen later on. The Bakhar, a translation of which is contained in Prof. Forrest's Selections from Bombay State Papers, Vol. I, must, it seems to me, have been in some parts mistranslated, and in all abridged in the translation. The original is hardly likely, for instance, to have spoken of a night darker than Shiváji's heart. (See p. 15)—a phrase which one would not expect to occur in relation to Shiváji in a Maráthá Bakhar deposited in Râigad.

(7) Bernier in his Travels (see new edition in Constable's Oriental Miscellany, pp. 220-1) and Ovington in his Voyage to Surat (pp. 189-228) afford some indication about the large armies maintained in those days and the expenses which their maintenance entailed.

(8) Grant Duff, Vol. I, p. 223 *et seq.*

Maráthá History, except during the régime of that excellent Péshwá, the elder Mádhavráv. (9) One principal feature of Shiváji's system consisted in the creation of a Cabinet Council—the famous Ashta Pradhân—or Eight Ministers. (10) And one of these eight was known as Panditráv. (11) His functions, like

(9) See about him Grant Duff, Vol. II, p. 208 *et seq*. and compare Forrest's Bombay Selections, Vol. I., p. 250; Fryer's Travels, pp. 79, 146.

(10) See Grant Duff, Vol. I, p. 235 *et seq*, comp. Chitragupta's Life of Shiváji, p. 103; Sabhâsad's ditto p. 69; and Vividhajnânavistâra, Vol. XIII, p. 238 *et seq*.; Forrest's Selections, pp. 14, 80.

(11) There is some diversity in the various accounts contained in our authorities about the institution of the Panditráv's office. The Maráthá Sámrájya Bakhar (p. 28) says, that it was established some little time after Shiváji's plunder of Surat, in order to provide an officer who would look after the grants made to Bráhmans with a view to the preservation of virtue and justice in the kingdom. Malhár Rámráv Chitnis seems to agree with this (see Vividhajnánavistára, Vol. X., p. 8), and to show that all Shiváji's administrative arrangements took shape at that time. Krishnáji Anant Sabhásad (p. 23) says that the title of Panditráv was bestowed on Raghunáth Pandit, when he was appointed as a fit and proper person for the negotiations with Mirzá Rájá Jayasing—an appointment which M. R. Chitnis also mentions. Chitragupta in his life (p. 105) and Gupté, the author of the Bhonslé Bakhar (p. 10), refer the institution of the office to the time of the Installation. See further as to the Panditráv's functions, M. R. Chitnis's Rájaniti pp. 10, 30, and compare Malcolm's Central India, Vol. II., p. 429; and Forbes's Oriental Memoirs, Vol. I., p. 214. (*Quœre* what is the meaning of JeiramOpput there mentioned? Can it be a proper name, Jayarám Bápat?) The Dhávadasi Bakhar mentions the Panditráv in connexion with the Svámi's funeral ceremonies.

those of the other Ministers and high officers, are stated in a Note or Memorandum which purports to be written on the 13th of Jyéshtha Vadya, Tuesday, of the first year of the era of Installation (A. D. 1674). (12) It states that the Panditráv's duties are to exercise all the ecclesiastical powers of the State, and to order punishment to be inflicted after investigating into what is and is not in accordance with the religious law. He is to receive learned persons on behalf of the State, and countersign all documents that may issue from the Sovereign relating to *Áchára*, *Vyavahára*, and *Prâyaschitta*, that is to say, rules of conduct, civil and criminal law, and penances (13), the three departments of the *Dharmashástra*. He is also to look after the performance of *Shântis* (14), and other ceremonials, and the distribution of the royal bounty. It is further stated in the Life of Shiváji, written by Malhár Rámráv Chitnis, that the scheme of the Cabinet and its functions was settled by Shiváji in conformity with previous practice and traditions (15).

---

(12) Letters, memoranda, &c., published, in the Kavyétihása Sangraha, p. 357.

(13) See West and Bühler's Hindu Law, p. 13.

(14) See Mandlik's Hindu Law. Intr. p. xxxii.

(15) Vividhajnánavistâra, Vol. XIII, pp. 201, 238; see also Sabhásad's Life of Shiváji, p. 69. At p. 725 of Mr. Forrest's Bombay Selections, Vol. I,

In an *Ajnápatra,* or Rescript, bearing date Márgashirsha Shudha 4th, Thursday of the forty-second year of the Installation era (1716 A. D.), issued by Rájá Shambhu Chhatrapati of Kolhápur, it is said that it is among the duties of a king of men to destroy any tendency towards impiety, and to increase piety, among his subjects, and thus to acquire eternal happiness in the life to come (16). Accordingly it is laid down (17) that heretical opinions, antagonistic to religion, should not by any means be allowed to prevail in the kingdom, and if perchance they should be found to have manifested themselves anywhere, the matter should be inquired into personally, that is to say, I understand, by the Minister himself to whom the order is directed, and due punishment should be inflicted, so that no one else may join in the evil courses, and they may ultimately be altogether stopped.

It would thus appear that the Maráthá Rájás considered it their right, or rather

---

is a translation of an essay by a Mahomedan writer of the last century, who alleges that Shiváji borrowed his scheme from the Musalmans. He does not mention any grounds for his statement.

(16) V. G. Vistâra, Vol. V, p. 194.

(17) Ditto, p. 91, and comp. Letters, &c., (K. I. Sangraha), p. 9.

their duty, to regulate the religious affairs of their subjects, although it is to be remarked, that the Minister appointed for the purpose of attending to this part of the Rájá's duties was in fact always a Bráhman, as indeed might naturally be expected. It further appears, that these duties were practically enforced, and did not exhaust themselves in being committed to paper. We find, for instance, that in the reign of Sambháji, the son and successor of Shiváji, the favourite "Kabji," (18) Kalushá, among his other high crimes and misdemeanours, induced the King, against the advice and remonstrance of the responsible Minister Panditráv, to order *Prâyaschittas* or penances, to be performed by eminent Bráhmans, "masters of six Shástrás" (19). What offences or shortcomings were alleged for justifying these orders, the document before

(18) The writer of the note at Dowson's Elliott, Vol. VII, p. 338, seems to be puzzled by this word; but it is, of course, equivalent to *kab* or *kavi* plus the honorific "ji. The Bhonslé Bakhar (p. 14), and M. R. Chitnis's Life of Sambháji (p. 7) and the Shri Shiva Kâvya, canto vi, st. 21, suggest that Kalushá was an emissary of Aurangzéb. See also Forbes' Oriental Memoirs, Vol. I., p. 462. The Mahomedan account, summarized in Dowson's Elliott (*loc. cit.*) does not support this suggestion; while it connects Kabji with the Bráhman Kásipant) in whose charge Sambháji had been left by Shiváji on his flight from Delhi.

(19) Maráthi Sámrájyáchi Bakhar, p. 59.

us does not state, and there is no other source of information on the subject known to me.

In the time of Sháhu again, when Báláji Bájiráo was Péshwá, the State had to deal with a dispute even then of long standing between the Bráhmans and the Prabhus (20). The dispute appears to have commenced as early as the days of Shiváji, (21), and the settlement then arrived at was, apparently, adhered to during the reigns of Sambháji and Rájárám, and the greater part of the reign of Sháhu himself. Towards the latter end of Sháhu's reign, however, the dispute was rekindled, as the Prabhus were much in favour with Sháhu as they had been with Shiváji (22). The Bráhmans of the day are charged, in the Prabhu chronicles, with having interpolated new verses into old Puránic and other books like the *Sahyâdri Khanda,* for the purpose of lowering the status of the Prabhu caste. The disputes having come before Báláji Bájiráo, the Péshwá, he wrote to Sháhu,

(20) This is the correct mode of spelling the name of the caste as claimed by themselves. The change to Parbhu (corrupted by Anglo-Indians to Purvoe) they attribute to jealousy. See Káyastha Prabhûnchi Bakhar, p. 6.

(21) See K. P. Bakhar (K. P. I. S.), pp. 10-12.

(22) See Chitragupta's Shiváji, p. 123.

recommending that the old practice should be adhered to, that the new quarrels raised by the Bráhmans should be discountenanced, and that they should be given final and clear orders in the matter. Sháhu (23) thereupon sent an order to all the Bráhmans of Khande and Máhuli (on the banks of the river Krishná) ordering that they should continue to perform all ceremonies, funeral and other, as the same had been theretofore performed, during the régime of the Bijapur Emperors, (24) and also in the time of Shiváji, Sambháji, Rájárám and Tárábái, and in the early days of the then current reign. They were directed "not to do anything new, not to break anything old." At the same time with this order of the Sovereign, the Panditráv Raghunáth appears also to have addressed a communication to the Bráhmans aforesaid, reciting briefly the order made by Sháhu, and adding that the old practice should be revived. (25) We learn, however, that although these orders were sent, the disputes were not in fact settled, as the Pratinidhi Jagjivanráv

---

(23) See K. P. Bakhar (K. P. I. S.), pp. 12-17.

(24) It seems to follow from this, that the Musalman Rájás had also dealt with the questions between these two castes.

(25) See K. P. Bakar (K. P. I. S.) pp. 12-13, where the letters are set out at length.

Pandit, and his agent Yamáji, who were managing all affairs at Sátárá on behalf of Sháhu, would not accept the settlement, seeing that Sháhu's end was approaching. Subsequently Sháhu died, as was expected, and Báláji Bájiráv immediately placed both the Pratinidhi and his agent Yamáji (26) in prison, and ordered (27) the old practice as regards ceremonies among Prabhu families to be resumed. That practice, then, continued undisturbed until the end of the administration of Mádhavráv, and the beginning of that of Náráyanráv.

Many years after this, (28) in the days of the Péshvá Savái Mádhavráv, a Bráhman, we learn, named Narhari Ranalekar became *yavanamaya* and *bhrashta*, which I understand to mean converted to Mahomedanism and fallen off from Hinduism. He was then taken back into the fold by certain Bráh-

---

(26) See Grant Duff, Vol. II, pp. 17, 32.

(27) Grant Duff, Vol. II, p. 35. The Panipat Bakhar of Raghunáth Yádav states (p. 7) that Sháhu on his death-bed made over the whole kingdom to Báláji Bájiráv.

(28) See Letters, Memoranda, &c. (K. I. Sangraha), p. 76. A similar question arose long afterwards in connection with the case of Srîpat Séshádri—a brother of the late Rev. Nárávan Séshádri—in which the late enlightened Prof. Bál Gangádhar Shástri is understood to have taken a prominent part which mortally offended the orthodoxy of his day.

mans of Paithana, although, as the Péshvá's order says, this was an unwarrantable proceeding. His re-admission led to a split in the Bráhman community of the place; and then an officer of the Government came upon the scene, and by coercion got all the Bráhmans, the excommunicated ones and the others, to sit down to dinner together. The result, says the Péshvá's order, was that the whole of the Paithana Bráhmans became excommunicated. And theretore the Sarkár, or Government, sent two Kárkuns to administer penance wholesale to all the Bráhmans of Paithana; and this was accordingly done. The order, then, which is addressed to the Déshmukhs and Déshpándés of Parganá Jálnápur, after reciting all this, directs that the other Bráhmans of the Parganá, having had intercourse with the Paithana Bráhmans, must also perform due penance, according to the measure of their intercourse, through the instrumentality of the two Government Kárkuns aforesaid. This case presents several remarkable features, not the least remarkable of which is the severe logic by which the penance is made to extend to all the Bráhmans of a whole Parganá. The same severe logic may be noticed in a later case, which occurred in October 1800—soon after the deaths of Náná Fadanavis and Parshurám

Bháu Patvardhan. It seems then to have been found out, that one of the household attendants in the Péshvá's palace, who had been supposed to be a Bráhman, was in fact of a low caste—a saddler. The man was ordered to be punished, and penance was administered to the whole city of Poona, that is, presumably, to the Bráhmans of the place, who must have been then, as they are now, the large majority of the inhabitants. (29)

A curious ecclesiastical case was disposed of by Sadáshivráv Bháu (30) at Trimbakéshvar. The Giri and Puri (31) sects of Gosávis had some dispute about bathing at Trimbakéshvar in the *Sinhastha* year—a dispute, apparently, about which of them was to have precedence. The dispute led, we are told, to severe fights, until Sadáshivráv having offered to settle the matter "on the part

(29) Letters, Memoranda &c. (K. I. Sangraha) p. 523. I know of no other source of information regarding the matter than the very short entry there. A curious extension of the severity of this logic even to deceased persons is suggested at Kayastha Prabhúnchyá Itihásáchin Sádhánén (Grámanya) p. 9. See further Letters, Memoranda &c. (K. I. Sangraha) p. 9. The passage there is rather obscure.

(30) It seems that Sadáshivráv principally managed the Péshvá's affairs, Báláji as a rule "taking it easy." See *inter alia* Forrest's Bombay Selections, Vol. I, pp. 121, 134, and compare Asiatic Researches, Vol. III, p. 91.

(31) See Prof. H. H. Wilson's Religious Sects of the Hindus, Vol. I, pp. 202-3.

of the Government," the two parties agreed, and then Sadáshivráv taking hold of the hands of the Mahants of the two rival sects, entered the sacred waters of the Kusávarta with the two Mahants for his companions. The two thus entering the water together, all disputes about precedence ceased. (32)

The Péshvá, however, had not been equally successful in settling another dispute between rival Bráhmans, (33) which had arisen some time before at Trimbakéshvar, in relation to the temple built by him at that place. The consecration of the edifice could not be performed at the time when Báláji wished it to be performed, because the Yajurvédi and Ápastamba Bráhmans had some dispute—the nature of which is not more precisely indicated—in connection with the southern gate of the Temple. (34) How the matter was ultimately settled does not appear. (35)

---

(32) See Péshvá's Bakhar, pp. 68-9.

(33) For another unsuccessful interference, or rather a series of unsuccessful interferences, by the State in ecclesiastical affairs, see the Káyastha Prabhûnchi Bakhar, p. 13 *et seq.*; Kayastha Prabhûnchyá Itihásáchin Sadhánén (Grámanya) p. 5 *et seq.*

(34) Péshvá's Bakhar pp. 68-9.

(35) But it appears from Letters, Memoranda, &c. (K. I. Sangraha), p. 522, that the consecration of the Trimbakéshvar Temple was made by Bájiráo II in Saka 1728 (A. D. 1806). The delay seems unaccountably long in spite of the difficulties raised by the Bráhmans.

It may be remarked, in passing, that some of the stone used under the orders of the Péshvá for erecting the Trimbakéshvar Temple, is stated to have been taken from the Mahomedan Musjids or Mosques in the Moghul districts. Whether such mosques were then unused and dilapidated or not does not appear. (36)

Another matter, in which the Péshvá of the day failed to carry out his own wishes, in consequence of opposition from the people, was one which had occurred in the time of the first Bájiráo. I have not seen any original authority for this, but a note of the Editor of the Péshvá's Bakhar says, that Bájiráo having had a son by the Musalman woman Mastâni, wanted to perform the thread-ceremony of that son and make a Bráhman of him; but that the plan fell through in consequence of the opposition of the Bráhmans. (37) In a sketch of the career of Bájiráo, bearing date in 1840,

(36) Péshvá's Bakhar p. 68. And compare *inter alia* Dowson's Elliot, Vol. VII, pp. 404, 415, 446, 456, and Malcolm's Central India, Vol. I, p. 56.

(37) Péshvá's Bakhar, p. 40. That such an idea should have occurred to a Hindu defender of the faith is itself rather remarkable as an example of that relaxation of old traditions adverted to further on in this paper And compare Grant Duff, Vol. I, p. 599. Well might Grant Duff say that Bájiráo was free from "bigotry"!

(though this is probably the date of the copy, not of the original sketch itself), a brief account is given of the sort of quasi-marriage, which had been celebrated between Bájiráo and Mastáni. (38) The account there given is that Mastáni was the daughter of the Nabáb of Hyderábád, that is to say, the Nizám, and that the Nabáb's wife suggested that their daughter might be married to Bájiráo, as a means of cementing friendship between them. The marriage was accordingly celebrated, but with a dagger; (39) and Bájiráo afterwards brought Mastáni away, and kept her in a separate mansion built specially for her in a part of the grounds of the Shanavár palace at Poona.

One matter of considerable importance, to which attention is being directed among

---

(38) Letters, Memoranda, &c. (K. I. Sangraha), p. 539. The whole story is a curious one, and there are sundry discrepancies in the various accounts we have of the transaction. See Shrì Sivakáyva, canto X, st. 58; Maráthi Sámrájya Bakhar, pp. 74-77; Kashiráj's Bhonslé Bakhar, p. 40; Péshvá's Bakhar pp. 37-40, see also p. 49; Péshvá's Shakávali, p. 6; Raghunáth Yádav's Pánipat Bakhar, p. 48; Chitni's Sháhu, p. 76; Forrest's Selections, p. 658. As to Sumshér Bahádur, the son of Mastáni. and the manner in which he was treated, and the designation he bore in relation to the Péshvá's family, see Forrest. p. 102. and Dowson's Elliott, Vol. VIII, p. 283, and compare Péshvás' Bakhar p. 150.

(39) As to this compare *inter alia*, Malcolm's Central India, Vol. II, p. 158.

Hindus at the present day, was dealt with by an order of the Péshvás--which of them was then in power it is not possible to say. The order provides, that no Bráhman in Prant Vái should accept a money payment for giving his girl in marriage; that whoever receives any money should forfeit double the amount of it to Government; whoever pays any should forfeit as much; and whoever may act as go-between in arranging such a marriage and receive money for his services as such should forfeit the amount of his brokerage. The official to whom the order is conveyed is directed to communicate the terms of it "in an emphatic manner" to all the Bráhman caste, and to all Jamindárs, ecclesiastical functionaries, officiating priests, astrologers (Joshis), and to pátils and kulkarnis; and he is ordered to recover the amounts as prescribed without listening to any pretext about expenses, &c. The letter now published acknowledges receipt of this order, the whole of which it recites; and promises to communicate it to the people of the town of Vái and of Government villages, and to Déshmukhs and Déshpándés. It is unnecessary to say anything more with reference to this order, than that its all-embracing character deserves notice. All parties to the nefarious transaction are hit at, the man who sells his girl, the man who buys her, and the man who arranges the bargain and sale. (40)

It would thus appear, that under Maráthá rule, the union of Church and State was very close indeed; that it was not merely a theoretical but a practically enforced union; and that it was so, as well during the regime of the Maráthá Rájás, as under that of the Bráhman Péshvás, though it is to be observed, *valeat quantum*, that the order of the Péshvá last mentioned bears the usual seal containing the name of Rájá Sháhu. (41) This is not much to be wondered at, considering that the idea of a State leaving all ecclesiastical and religious affairs outside its own jurisdiction, is not one which is

(40) See Letters, Memoranda, &c. (K. I. Sangraha) pp. 121-2. Manu, chap. III, st. 51 *et seq* and chap. IX, st. 98 *et seq.* forbids what he in terms stigmatizes as a sale of a daughter, and the established name for the transaction in Maráthi still is Kanyâvikraya or sale of a daughter. See also Manu, chap. XI, 62 *et seq.* It will be seen that the particular sanctions enacted by the Péshvá are not such as can be found in the Manu Smriti, and so far the Pèshvá's order is in its nature, legislative, to borrow a term appertaining to the conceptions of the present day.

(41) In the Káyastha Prabhûnchi Bákhar, p. 12, is a letter from the Péshvá making a recommendation, and one from the Rájá issuing the required orders through the Panditráv.

even now universally accepted, and considering further that the main inspiring principle of the whole movement initiated by Shiváji and carried on by his successors down to the closing years of the Péshvá régime was the preservation of the Hindu religion against foreign aggression. (42) The only point one is struck by is that the Maráthá Rájás should have been prepared and able to meddle so far as they did in religious matters. One possible explanation is that the people at large may have accepted the claims made in favour of Shiváji's *Kshatriya* origin—a matter on which something more will have to be said in the sequel. On the other hand, it is to be observed that the Shástris generally have been chary of admitting, and in fact have often expressly denied, (43) the existence of any castes

(42) See *inter alia* Sabhásad's Life, pp. 27-8; V. J. Vistára. Vol. IX, pp. 50-3; Maráthi Sámrájya Bakhar, p. 76, Bhonslé's Bakhar, p. 7; Bhonslé Letters, Memoranda, &c. (K. I. Sangraha), p. 147; Nigudkar's Life of P. B. Patvardhan, p. 87; Malcolm's Central India, Vol. I. p. 69.

(43) See *inter alia* West and Bühler's Digest of Hindu Law, p. 921 note. The learned authors of that work, Sir R. West and Dr. J. G. Bühler, had seen a large number of opinions of Shástris recorded in the various British Courts in the Bombay Presidency. The Shástris in other parts of the country also have, on various occasions, expressed opinions to the same effect. They may be seen referred to in the report of a case decided by Her Majesty's Privy

other than Bráhmans and Sudrás at the present day. They have generally, I believe, relied on an old text of the Bhágavata Purána, (44) which says that the Nandás were the last of the Kshatriyás; and they have not, as far as I am aware, grappled, from that standpoint, with the claims of Shiváji to rank as a Kshatriya—claims, which appear to have been at least acquiesced in by Rámadása. (45) Another explanation may,

---

Council at Moore's Indian Appeal Cases, Vol. VII, pp. 35-7, 46-9. Steel is there quoted as showing that the claims to Kshatriya descent of the Bhonslés and other Maráthá families have been denied; and that the denial is based, not on the passage of the Bhágavata referred to in the text, but on the extinction of the Kshatriyás by Parashurama. But it is obvious that this last argument proves too much. For if it is correct, what is to be said of the caste status of Ráma of Ayodhyá, to take only one instance, and the series of his successors as described, for example in Kálidása's Raghuvansa? See further Malcolm's Central India, Vol. I, p. 43.

(44) One explanation of this text, which I believe to be the usual one, applies it only to the land of Magadha, not the whole of Bharatakhanda. For another explanation, given by Benáres Pandits, see Káyastha Prabhûnchi Bakhar, p. 17.

(45) See *inter alia* Dásabodha XIII, 6. Hémádri, too, describes the Jádhav prince, Mahádéva, as of the Somavansa, and as having performed Yajnás. At V. J. Vistára, Vol. IX, p. 35, it is said that the Maráthás are Rajputs with only altered names. See also as to this, Journal Bom. Br. Roy. As. Society, Vol. IX, p. CXLIV; and compare, Bhonslé Bakhar, pp. 3-5; M. R. Chitnis's Rájaniti, p. 7; Forrest's Selections, p. 726; Dowson's Elliott, Vol. VII, p. 254; Vol. VIII, p. 258.

perhaps, be found in the old doctrine that every king has more or less of the divine element in him. In one passage of one of our recently published Bakhars, no less a person than the Moghul emperor of Delhi has been given the benefit of that doctrine. (46) And if that is allowable, *a fortiori* must Shiváji and Sambháji be also allowed to be entitled to a share of the quasi-divine character. (47)

At this point, I cannot resist the temptation to draw attention to a passage in

---

(46) The passages relating to this point are all extremely curious, and deserve to be examined in their original places. See Pánipat Bakhar by R. Yádav, pp. 19-20; Chitnis's Rájárám I, p. 71; Bháu Sáhéb's Bakhar, p. 56; Chitraguptá's Shiváji, p. 137; Chitnis's Rájârám II, p. 55; Sri Sivakávya, canto 1, st. 119; Compare Letters, &c., p. 37, see also Forbes's Oriental Memoirs, Vol. III. 149, (which shows that Akbar was regarded as a divine incarnation), and Dowson's Elliot, Vol. V., pp. 569-70. In Dowson's Elliot, Vol. VII. p. 284, we are told that there was in Delhi a sect of Hindus, who did not take their daily food until after they had "Darsana" of Aurangzéb, and were thence called Darsanis!

(47) See Chitnis's Rájaniti, p. 123; Chitraguptá's Shiváji, pp. 5, 16, 32, 41, 101; Khardá Bakhar, p. 22. In the Káyastha Prabhûnchyá Itihâsâchin Sádhanén (Grámanya) p. 5, it is stated, that when the dissensions between the Bráhmans and Prabhus were going on in the life-time of Náráyanráv Péshvá, the champions of the former said: "What does it matter what is in the Shástrás? Who looks at them? The Péshvás are sovereigns. It is necessary to act as they direct." Tavernier, Vol. I. p. 356 shows a similar complacency on the part of Mahomedan Doctors of the Law in presence of Aurangzéb. And see also Bernier, p. 288.

Krishnáji A. Sabhásad's Life of Shiváji. Although, as above stated, his movement was in essence a religious one, it appears that in providing for the preservation of temples and religious institutions of his own faith, (48) Shiváji also continued the existing grants in favour of Musalman Pirs, mosques, &c, for keeping up lights (49) and religious services. As Sabhásad's Life professes to have been written at the desire of Rájárám, the second son of Shiváji, in 1694, and as there is some internal evidence to confirm this claim, the information furnished by

---

(48) See Sabhásad's Life, p. 27; Chitragupta, p. 40; V. J. Vistára, Vol. IX, p. 36; Fryer's Travels, p. 68, and Bernier, pp. 188-9, afford independent confirmation of these statements. And Dowson's Elliott, Vol. VII, p. 260, is of special value, as coming from a Mahomedan source. This tolerance sometimes was carried too far; see *inter alia* Maráthi Sámrájya Bakhar p. 14. (see also the curious story at p. 48); M. R. Chitnis's Sambháji, p. 5; Holkar's Kaifiyat, p. 108 (where the Holkar takes the "Fakiri," a matter still not uncommon), Forrest's Selections p. 1; Forbes's Oriental Memoirs, Vol. II, pp. 118, 255. With this may be compared Mahomedan liberality as shown in the prohibition of cow-slaughter procured by Mahádji Sindhiá from the Delhi Emperor. See Grant Duff, Vol. III, p. 76; Malcolm's Central India, Vol. I, pp. 164, 194. And see also Bernier, pp. 306, 326. The Portuguese are stated to have been very intolerant; see the Sáshti Bakhar, p. 1; Dowson's Elliott, Vol., VII, pp. 211, 345; Ovington's Voyage to Surat, p. 206.

(49) As to this compare Scott's Deccan, Vol. I, p. 203. Fryer's Travels, p. 124.

Shiváji's biographer is obviously of great historic value.

To return, however, to our main point. In connection with this ecclesiastical jurisdiction, it may be useful to note, that it is clear from the *Káyastha Prabhûnchi Bakhar*, (50) that the Musalman sovereigns of Bijápur were also on occasion called on to deal with these ecclesiastical cases arising among their Hindu subjects. It appears, for instance, that in the course of the quarrels between the Bráhmans and Prabhus in the Konkan, the two parties once went to the local Bijápur officer for redress. He was a Musalman, and he pointed out that he knew nothing of the *shástrás* of the litigants. He therefore told them both to go to their principal sacred place, Benáres, and obtain a decision from the Pandits there; and promised that he would enforce such decision. The Bakhar goes on to say, that the parties did accordingly repair to Benáres, where a great *sabhá* or assembly of the Pandits was held,

(50) pp. 8-9. At a later stage of these disputes, in the days of Náná Fadanavis's power, the Prabhus said "all our caste prays for an assembly of Pandits to be convened to determine our status. Then let an order of the State be issued, and it will be our duty to have the ceremonies performed as ordered. Only let the State orders be given after due consideration." Káyastha Prabhûchyá Itihásáchin Sâdhanén (Grámanya) p. 17; K. P. Bakhar, p. 12.

and after high debate it was determined that the Prabhus were genuine Kshatriyás, and entitled to the benefit of Védic ceremonies, (51) and to be taught the sacred *Gáyatri* verse. The Bráhmans are said to have been satisfied, and to have agreed to conduct the ceremonies for the Prabhus in the regular manner. And it is stated subsequently that this was accordingly done.

Perhaps the incidents relating to the marriage of Shaháji may be looked at as affording another illustration of the same character. The incidents are curious on other grounds also, and may, therefore, be fitly set out at some length. (52) Máloji, the father of Shaháji, and his brother Vithoji, were both employed in the service of Lukj Jádhavráv, a Mansabdár under the Nizámsháhi Government. On one occasion, in 1598, when the *Shimgá* festivities of the *Ranga* were being celebrated at the house of Jádhavráv, Máloji and his young son Shaháji being present, the host seated Shaháji, then five years of age and a handsome looking boy, by the side of his daughter,

(51) As to this see West and Bühler's Digest of Hindu Law, p. 920 ; but see also Mandlik's Hindu Law, p. 56.

(52) See Maráthi Sámrájya Bakhar, pp. 4-7, and compare V. J. Vistára, Vol. IX, p. 37 *et seq*, also Grant Duff, Vol. I, p.

who was three years old. And in the course of conversation he happened to remark, as people often do on such occasions, that the two would make a very suitable match, and asked the girl if she would like to have Shahaji for her husband. Immediately Máloji and his brother Vithoji declared to the assembled guests that the word of Jádhavráv had been passed in favour of the match, and called on them to bear witness to the fact. Jádhavráv's wife, however, would not consent to this, and she got him to dismiss Máloji and Vithoji. They both left, but after some time they appear to have prospered, and to have placed themselves at the head of a body of two or three thousand soldiers, and also to have got help from others. They then went to a place near Daulatábád, and threw some slaughtered pigs into the mosque there with letters addressed to the Nizám, stating the contract between them and Jádhavráv, and threatening that if the king did not arrange for the marriage being celebrated in pursuance of the contract, they would desecrate (53) other mosques in the same way. The Nizám at once took up the matter, and directed Já-

(53) For a funny story of an Englishman's revenge on a Musalman, in which pig's flesh plays an important part, see Tavernier's Travels by V. Ball, Vol. I, p. 11.

dhavráv to carry out the contract of marriage. This was ultimately done with great pomp under the auspices of the Nizám himself, who took Máloji and Vithoji into his own service. The proceedings connected with this affair are, it need hardly be remarked, altogether of a curious and irregular character, but they appear to indicate that even in the delicate affairs of marriage, recourse was had by the Hindu subjects of Musalman Kings to the assistance of their Sovereigns, in whatever way such assistance might be invoked.

There is a passage in the Bakhar of the battle of Khardá, which illustrates how this ecclesiastical jurisdiction was sometimes invoked, and how it was practically worked on its judicial side. At Talégáum, it seems, there was a Bráhman woman, who lived in adultery with a Musalman. (54) The Bráhmans of the place made a complaint about this to Náná Fadanavis at Poona, stating the facts, and adding, in the usual style, that the days of Bráhmanism were gone! Náná expressed his disbelief in the charge, but appointed a *Panch* or board ot arbitrators to investigate it. (55) The *Panch*

(54) See the Khardá Bakhar, pp. 5-6. (Grant Duff's spelling of the name, Kurdla, is incorrect.)

(55) As to this mode of administering criminal justice see Grant Duff, Vol. II, p. 237, compare Forbes' Oriental Memoirs, Vol. I, p. 474; Malcolm's

were apparently bribed by the Musalman, and even before the time for final decision was reached, betrayed a tendency to decide in the Musalman's favour, holding that the charge was false. Thereupon "a hundred or two hundred Bráhmans" gathered together and went up to Poona. There they went before the tent of the Péshvá, (who was starting with his army on the expedition which ended at Khardá), and sat there in the middle of the day with torches blazing. When the Péshvá came out of the tent, the Bráhmans set up a loud cry: "Har! Har! Mahádév!" And on the Péshvá desiring to know the meaning of it all, they said they had come from Talégáum, stated their whole case, and explained that they had lighted torches at midday, as there was so much darkness, that is, absence of justice, prevailing in the kingdom. Náná was thereupon sent for, and subsequently the arbitrators, and finally the accused woman. The woman on being asked at first remained silent. But cane sticks being ordered to be

---

Central India, Vol. I, p. 536; Vol. II, pp. 290, 426; Stephen's Impey and Nandkumár, Vol. I, p. 247; Vol. II, p. 78. As to what is said by Grant Duff about women and Bráhmans not being put to death, compare M R. Chitnis's Life of Sháhu the younger, pp. 72-80; Péshvá's Bakhar, p. 132; Forrest p. 18; Chitraguptá's Shiváji p. 5; Chitnis's Sháhu I, pp. 25, 5; Sambháji, pp. 12, 14.

sent for (56) she acknowledged her guilt, and the Péshvá thereupon decided that both the accused persons were guilty--a decision in which Yajnésvar Shástri is stated to have concurred. The sentence was that the male culprit was ordered first to be paraded through the streets of Poona on the back of a donkey with his face turned towards the back (57) of the animal, and then tied to the foot of an elephant and killed; and the female culprit, as she could not be sentenced to death, (58) was banished from the kingdom.

---

(56) This is in accordance with old tradition, compare Mudrârâkshasa, Act V; Wilson's Hindu Theatre, Vol. I. p. 201.

(57) See Scott's Deccan, Vol. I, p. 375.

(58) See note 55 supra. The punishments here mentioned were in use in those days for divers offences. The infamous Ghásirâm Kotvál was subjected to the parade called Dhinda (See Péshvá's Bakhar p. 157), though he appears to have had a camel instead of a donkey to ride on. But see Forbes Oriental Memoirs Vol. II. p. 135, where the whole affair is described at length. See also Fryer p. 97. Some of Náráyanráv Péshvá's murderers, and the pretender Sadáshivráv Bháu (Grant Duff's spelling of this name as Sewdasheorao is incorrect) were tied to the feet of elephants and thus killed. (See Bháusáhéb's Kaifiyat p. 3; and compare Forrest's Selections p. 4, Dowson's Elliott Vol. VII. pp. 359-63, Bernier's Travels p. 177, Scott's Deccan Vol. I pp. 134, 285, 393, and Hamilton's East Indies, Vol. I. p. 178, where it is said that this was esteemed an ignominious death.) Others were beheaded or shot. And some had torches tied to their persons, which then were lighted, and they were thus burnt to

The various incidents to which we have thus referred illustrate the ecclesiastical jurisdiction of the Maráthá sovereigns in all aspects. We see from them that those sovereigns, as heads alike of the State and the Church, to borrow a Christian expression, exercised legislative powers, judicial powers both by themselves and through the medium of arbitrators, administrative powers by a departmental Minister, and executive powers through the instrumentality of Government Kárkuns. And the documents, it may be added, which furnish this information, extend over nearly the whole period of Maráthá rule, from the time of Shiváji down to that of Savái Mádhavráv.

It has been already stated, that the Maráthá Rájás who claimed and exercised the wide ecclesiastical jurisdiction thus indicated in outline, were regarded as Kshatriyás. The recently published documents contain many allusions to this point. But from those which

---

death, after their fingers had been pierced with needles. See Péshvá's Bakhar p. 132. For different and varying accounts of the pretender Sadáshivráv's death, see Péshvá's Bakhar p. 134, and Nigudkar's Life of Parashurám Bháu Patvardhan p. 40, and Grant Duff Vol. II. pp. 331-5. Péshvá's Shakâvalî p. 30; Dawson's Elliott Vol. VIII 294, Maráthi Sámrájya Bakhar p. 100, and Chitnis's Rájárám p. 45.

relate to Shiváji himself, (59) it rather appears, if we read between the lines, that the claim set up on his behalf to be of the *Kshatriya* caste was not universally regarded as really and truly tenable, although from considerations of policy and expediency it might be conceded. From the Biographies of Shiváji, by Krishnáji Anant Sabhásad, (60) and by Chitragupta, (61) it seems to follow that the search for the origin of Shiváji's family, which resulted in the discovery that he belonged to the Sisode (62) clan of Rajputs who reigned in Udayapur, (63) was not commenced until after the idea of a formal installation (or *Abhishéka*) had been started. And Malhár Rámráo Chitnis's narrative,

(59) See *inter alia* Chitraguptá's Life pp. 108, 116 168 and compare Maráthi Sâmrâjya Bakhar p. 47.

(60) See p. 68. See also Forrest's Selections p. 22.

(61) P. 98.

(62) See V. J. Vistâra, Vol. X, pp. 44, 116-9.

(63) See Chitnis's Sháhu p. 9; see too V. J. Vistâra Vol. IX. p. 32; Gupté's Bhonslé Bakhar p. 4; Letters, Memoranda &c. (K. I. Sangraha) p. 362; M. R. Chitnis's Life of Sháhu the Younger pp. 101-2, where the different practice of the old Udayapur family in a certain matter of ceremonial is referred to. It will be remembered, that the Udayapur family were the oldest of the Rajput clans (See Grant Duff, Vol. I, p. 27) and that they were the only family which had not permitted a daughter of theirs to marry into the family of the great Moghul. (See. Elphinstone's India, by Cowell, pp. 480-506-7, and compare V. J. Vistára Vol. IX p. 29, Bernier's Travels p. 126 n., Dowson's Elliott Vol. VII, pp. 195-6.

although it proceeds on the assumption of the fact as already established, rather indicates that Gágábhatta, the great Pandit of Benáres, whose services were put in requisition for the installation ceremonies, had some considerations of policy put to him before he was persuaded to join in those ceremonies. (64) They had also to strain a point, when as a preliminary to the installation, the thread ceremony essential for a Kshatriya, was performed on Shiváji at a time when he was "forty-six or fifty years old" and had already had two sons—an irregularity, which also was, we are told, expressly assented to by all the Bráhmans and Pandits. (65) How the Bráhmans and Pandits worked their way to this decision, none of our authorities states. Further, it is remarkable that none of those authorities anywhere mentions the performance of the thread ceremony upon any of the members of Shiváji's family, except the ones who were installed on the gadi, (66) and then that

(64) V. J. Vistára, Vol. XIII, p. 202. See the history of the Chitnis family (K. P. I. S.) pp. 6-8 and Káyastha Prabhunchi Bakhar pp. 10-1. According to a writer in the Jnána Prakásh newspaper of Poona, Gágá bhatta used the argument from expediency to recon cile the people to what was being done. No authority is quoted for this version of the affair.

(65) See V. J. Vistára Vol. XIII. p. 203.

(66) Rájárám's is mentioned by M. R. Chitnis, V. J. Vistára, Vol. XIII, p. 248. (Sambháji's thread

ceremony is mentioned only in connection with the installation ceremony. (67) In view of these facts, it may be permissible to doubt whether the statements of both Krishnáji Anant Sabhásad (68) and Malhár Rámráo Chitnis, about Shaháji claiming to be a Rajput of the Sisode clan, or about Jayasing Mirzá Rájá of Jeypore acknowledging Shiváji as a *Kshatriya* and dining with him before the installation, deserve to be entirely trusted. (69) That at a later time the Sátárá Rájás, (70) the Sindiá (71) and the Nágpur Bhonslés and Ghorpadés and others claim to be *Kshatriyás* is a matter which after Shiváji's affairs need excite no

---

ceremony appears to have taken place at a much earlier age than Shiváji's; apparently it was celebrated as a preliminary to his installation as Yuvarája or heir apparent).

(67) *e.g.* See Chitnis's Life of Rájárám II. p. 2. Life of Sháhu, p. 16.

(68) Sabhásad's Life pp. 28, 38. See V. J. Vistára, Vol. IX, p. 30; Vol. X, pp. 44, 119; Vol. XIII, p. 202, where Shiváji claims that other members of his family are reigning in Cutch and Népál.

(69) See too Chitnis's Sháhu pp. 9, 61; and Rájárám II, p. 2. In Forbes's Oriental Memoirs we are told that the Maráthás, "are accounted among the lower tribes of the Hindus," Vol. I, p. 459, Vol. II, p. 61; and compare Dowson's Elliott, Vol. VIII, p. 209.

(70) See Maráthi Sámrájya Bakhar p. 116; and the references already given; compare also Scott's Deccan, Vol. I, p. 32; Vol. II, p. 4; Forrest's Selections p. 725.

(71) See Bháu Sáhéb's Bakhar, p. 68.

surprise. The explanation of it all is contained in a passage in K. A. Sabhásad's Life. He says that Gágábhatta (72) was much pleased with the splendid reception given him by Shiváji; and it was he who suggested that while a Musalman Pádshá sat on the throne, and had the *chhatra* or umbrella indicative of sovereignty, (73) it was not proper that Shiváji, who had achieved what he had, should not adopt the formal ensigns of kingship. (74) And it was when this suggestion was accepted by Shiváji, and a formal *Abhishéka* determined on, that it became necessary to look into the origin of the family, and to promulgate that Shiváji was by birth a *Kshatriya*. Taking the whole evidence together, it looks like a case of a more or less deliberate manipulation of facts and religious rules, in aid of a foregone conclusion adopted for a purely political purpose. (75)

---

(72) Chitragupta (p. 95) appears to say that Gágábhatta had come of his own motion to see Shiváji. The other authorities point the other way. Gágábhatta is said to have got a lakh of rupees as a present. See Chitnis Family, p. 6 (K. P. I. S.)

(73) See Scott's Deccan, Vol. I, pp. 81, 93, 210, 288, 351, 370-6. The passage at p. 351 should be noted; and compare Ovington's Voyage to Surat p. 315.

(74) P. 30.

(75) Shiváji is stated to have been "rather keen about getting his *Munja*, or thread ceremony, per-

Of similar manipulations, or of more open and direct violations of religious rules of greater or less importance, the documents before us afford sundry other examples. One of the earliest occurred in connection with the arrangements for the accommodation of Sambháji, when Shiváji, after the flight from Delhi, was obliged, in order to disembarrass himself of all impediments, to leave the young prince behind him. It appears that some of Aurangzéb's people suspected that the boy was not, as pretended, a son of the Bráhman Káshipant, in whose charge he was. And in order to silence their suspicions, Káshipant was obliged to accept their challenge, and to eat out of the same dish as Sambháji. The Bráhman made the offence as light as he could make it, by taking a quantity of parched and flatten-

---

formed. See Chitraguptá's Life, p. 84. In the V. J. Vistára, Vol. XIII, p. 202, it is said that he consulted all and sundry upon that and kindred matters. It is also stated [See Maráthi Sámrájva Bakhar p. 47, and account of Bábá Sáhéb Gupté (K. P. I. S.) p. 8] that at one time Shiváji, after being taught the Gáyatri mantra (Om Tat Savitur &c.) was going in for the regular Bráhmanical life in preference to the Kshatriya (Compare Sri Siva Kávya, canto I, st. 50) But he subsequently allowed himself to be dissuaded from this by his officers. He then ordered that no mean employment was to be given to Bráhmans, and he made several transfers accordingly. See also Grant Duff, Vol. I, p. 266; Forrest's Selections, Vol. I, p. 251.

ed rice (76) (*Pohé*) mixed with curds on a plantain leaf (77), for the purpose of eating in the presence of Aurangzéb's myrmidons. These men made a favourable report to the Emperor, and Sambháji was saved. But one of Shiváji's biographers, Chitragupta, says that the Bráhman Káshipant secretly performed penance for what he had done. (78) It is to be remarked, that Sambháji is stated by the same writer to have been dressed like

---

(76) Compare Dowson's Elliott, Vol. VII, p. 285; See also *Ibid*. Vol. I, p. 9; V. J. Vistára, Vol. X. p. 200.

(77) Forbes, (Oriental Memoirs, Vol. II, p. 49) says that in his days a Bráhman might not eat out of tinned copper vessels, but had to use plantain leaves, &c.

(78) P. 75. Other authorities say nothing about any penance. This test of dining together appears to have been frequently applied in Maráthá History. See *inter alia* M. R. Chitnis's Life of Rájárám II, p. 2; Asiatic Researches, Vol. III, p. 137; Grant Duff, Vol. II, p. 39; Malcolm's Central India, Vol. II, pp. 131, 149; besides, Chitraguptá's Life, p. 62; Gáikavád's Kaifiyat p. 6; Maráthi Sámrájya Bakhar, p. 32; V. J. Vistára, Vol. IX, pp. 31-2, 70; Vol. X, p. 202; Gupté's Bhonslé Bakhar, pp. 9, 20, 31. For two curious incidents connected with dining together, see Holkar's Kaifiyat p. 4; Gupté's Bhonslé Bakhar, p. 31. A writer in the Jnána Prakásh of Poona says that when Rájárám and his attendants were moving about the country, Aurangzéb's people once encountered them; and in order to avoid their suspicions, Maráthás, Prabhus, and Bráhmans all sat down together to dinner in one row with silken clothes on. I have not seen this stated in any of the published Bakhars.

a Bráhman (79) with a *Dhotar* (80) tied round his waist, and also with the sacred thread, which he did not get as of right till about 1679, when Shiváji had his thread ceremony performed, with a view to instal him as *Yuvarája* or heir apparent. (81)

A somewhat similar occurrence had taken place before in Shiváji's family, on his father Shaháji's death, when in spite of the prayers of her son, Jijibái at first insisted on preparations being made for her sacrificing herself as a *Sati*. Chitraguptá's Life (82) shows,

---

(79) See Chitraguptá's Life, p. 77; V. J. Vistára, Vol. X, p. 185; Scott's Deccan, Vol. II. p. 16.

(80) Péshvá's Bakhar, pp. 105, 139, 143, shows that Bráhmans used trousers without much scruple. Savái Mádhavráv appears to have put them on on the occasion of his wedding. See also Chitraguptá's Shiváji, p. 5, Forbes's Oriental Memoirs, Vol. II, p. 12. In the Bhonslè Bakhar, p. 48, a change in the established fashion of the headdress is strongly objected to. It may be allowable, perhaps, to point out the parallel between this and the curious conservatism of an English lawyer mentioned in that most interesting work—Charles Sumner's Life and Letters, Vol. I, p. 338.

(81) See V. J. Vistára, Vol. X, p. 185; Maráthi Sámrájya Bakhar, p. 32; Bhonslé Bakhar p. 9; Chitraguptá's Shiváji, p. 77. At Dowson's Elliott, Vol. VII, p. 272, it is clearly implied that Sambháji had been married before going to Delhi. The contrary appears from V. J. Vistára, Vol. X, p. 303; Maráthi Sámrájya Bakhar, p. 117; see also V. J. Vistára, Vol. XIII, p. 342.

(82) See p. 85. Compare Sabhásad's Life, p. 55. See also Holkar's Kaifiyat, p. 67, and Bernier p. 308.

that the argument which ultimately prevailed with the lady was, that if she insisted on having her own way, Shiváji's life could not be relied on, and the empire established by him would at once cease to exist. Other instances of the same character are not wanting in subsequent years—in the days of the Péshvá power. The great violation of religious rules, which was involved in the Bráhman Péshwás taking to the military profession, is become so familiar and such a matter of course, so to say, that it hardly strikes one sufficiently as being a violation at all. (83) In the protest made by the eminent Rám Shástri against the Péshvá Mádhavráv's devoting too much time to religious observances, (84) their incompatibility with the duties of *Kshatriyás*, which the Péshvás had undertaken, is the strongest point in the argument; and the departure from the ordinances of the faith

---

(83) For what a Bráhman of our own day says about it, see V. J. Vistára, Vol. XXI, p. 284; also Sri Siva Kávya I, pp. 112-5, 121; II, pp. 49, 117. Compare Malcolm s Central India, Vol. I, p. 77; Forbes's Oriental Memoirs, Vol. II, p. 209; Forrest, p. 728. From Letters, Memoranda &c., (K. I. S.) p. 9, we learn, that the Péshvás had resorted to special religious ceremonials for obtaining sovereignty.

(84) Forbes (Oriental Memoirs, Vol. I, p. 472) speaks of Mádhavráo as "possessed of a mind unfettered by the restraints and superstitious tenets of the Hindus."

is assumed as an accomplished and irreversible fact, not a matter under discussion at all. (85) Another story, pointing the same way, is told of the same eminent Péshvá—Mádhavráv. When he was arranging for his expedition against Hyder Ali, he sent a summons in the usual way (86) to the Bhonslé Chief of Nágpur to come over to join the Maráthá army. The Bhonslé's agent at Poona went to consult the Ex-minister, Sakhárám Bápu, as to what should be done. The latter was afraid to give his counsel openly, as the Péshvá's Kárkun was present. But he managed to convey his advice to the Bhonslé's agent, without the Kárkun understanding the point. Sakhárám Bápu suggested to one of two persons who were sitting near him playing chess, that as the pawns (87) of his opponent had advanced in force, he should take back his king a square or two. The Bhonslé's agent, taking the hint, at once wrote off to his master to advise that he should not come to Poona in pursuance of the

(85) Grant Duff, Vol. II, p. 209.

(86) This formed the subject of special stipulations between the Péshvás and Bhonslés. See Bhonslé Letters &c. (K. I S.) pp. 23, 64, 65, 70, 114, and compare Chitnis's Rájárám, p. 23, Péshvá's Bakhar, p. 91.

(87) Pawns in Maráthi are called Pyádás which also means "soldiers."

Péshvá's summons, but should go back the one or two stages he had advanced from Nágpur. This was done accordingly, and Mádhavráv, who had a great reputation for obtaining news of everything that was going on in which he was interested, (88) heard of the Bhonslé's return to his capital, and also of Sakhárám Bápu's advice which led to it—though the latter was perceived only by him under the facts he learnt from the cross-examination of the Kárkun. Mádhavráv was a man of very strong will; he at once sent for the Bhonslé's agent, and told him of his master's return to Nágpur on the advice of Sakhárám Bápu, and added "If your master is in Poona within fifteen days, well and good: if not I will pay no heed to the fact of your being a Bráhman, (89)

---

(88) Náná Fadanavis is believed to have adopted and carried out Mádhavráv's system of obtaining news from everywhere. See Grant Duff, Vol. II, p. 229. It is one of the points specially noticed in Gopikábái's letter to Savái Mádhavráv; see Letters, Memoranda &c. (K. I. S.). p. 459. And as to Náná compare Péshvá's Bakhar, pp. 146-8 *inter alia.*

(89) See Péshvá's Bakhar, p. 94. For a more ferocious story, about Rághobá Dádá, see Péshvá's Bakhar, pp. 81-2. The Jnána Prakásh newspaper of Poona recently published another story with a similar moral. It appears that a Bráhman employé of the Péshvás, in the Military Department, accidentally discharged a gun and killed another Bráhman. The former was thereupon excommunicated for Bráhmanicide. But Rám Shástri, having regard to the fact

but will smash your head with a tent-peg (90)!"

The matter may, perhaps, be said to be carried a step further, when a Bráhman Kárkun, writing of the end of the Bráhman Parashurám Bháu Patvardhan's life, writes as follows (91): "The end of the deceased was excellent. For he served the Péshvás, performing a *Kshatriyá's* duties to the very last!" (92) But even if we pass from the cases of these secularised Bráhmans (93) as they may be called, we find in the instance of the priests of Kayagaum, and perhaps I may add of the Svámi of Dhávadasi, that these men while still living as religious Bráhmans, appear to have devoted themselves to worldly, that is, political, pursuits. About

---

of the death being accidental, publicly dined in company with the excommunicated Bráhman; and when asked for an explanation as to the authority for his proceeding, replied that it had the same authority as there was for associating with the Péshvás, who, though Bráhmans themselves, were answerable for many more heinous homicides!

(90) As to killing with a tent-peg, see Chitnis's Rájárám, p. 72; Maráthi Sámrájya Bakhar, p. 100; Péshvá Shakávali, p. 30; Holkar's Kaifiyat, p. 79.

(91) Letters, Memoranda &c. (K. I. S.), p. 501.

(92) This is nearly all reproduced in the Life of Bháu by Nigudkar recently published, p. 123. Compare also Pánipat Bakhar p. 42; and Bháu Sáhéb's Kaifiyat, p. 24.

(93) As to a Shástri transmogrified into a soldier see Chitnis's Rájárám, p. 104.

the latter I only know from oral information, the recently published Bakhar, and the note in Grant Duff's history (94). The original correspondence alluded to, I have not seen. But with regard to the former, the published letters show that they lent money at interest (95) to the Péshvás, were consulted by them about men and things connected with the State, and in fact took an active personal, if occasional, share in public affairs. (96)

Another point of the same sort may be noted, as being a somewhat remarkable one. Among the papers recently published is a letter addressed to the Péshvá Savái Mádhavráv, by his grandmother Gopikábái, in reply to a request by the former for advice as to how he should conduct himself. One of the directions given to her grandson by this old

(94) Grant Duff, Vol. I, p. 523 n.

(95) A वेदशास्त्रसंपन्न gentleman is mentioned at Letters, Memoranda &c. (K. I. S.), p. 395, as engaging in financial transactions.

(96) See Letters, Memoranda &c. (K. I. Sangraha) p. 2 *et seq.* In this connection the metamorphosis of Gosávis into soldiers may also be noted. See Grant Duff, Vol. III. pp. 33, 338, and cf *inter alia* Bháu Sáhèb's Kaifiyat, p. 23 ; Bháu Sáhèb's Bakhar, p 53 and Holkar's Kaifiyat, p. 53 ; Dowson's Elliott, Vol. VII, p. 294 ; Malcolm's Central India, Vol. II, p. 168 ; Forbes's Oriental Memoirs, Vol. II, p. 9, See also as to Bairágis, Holkar's Kaifiyat, pp. 7, 8, 62 ; Péshvá's Bakhar, p. 230.

lady, the widow of Báláji Bájiráv, was that he should cut short his *Sandhyá* worship, and that while the household priest performed the general daily worship of the household gods, he should only offer them the leaves of the *Tulasi* plant. Such a direction, given by a woman, and to a young boy who was only just learning to read, write and cipher, affords remarkable evidence of how the exigencies of the times were operating to relax the rigours of the old religious observances even in the family of the Péshvás. (97) Gopikábái was a very practical lady, of quick intelligence and strong will, (98) and must have seen the habitual course of life of several prominent men in the history of the Péshvá régime. (99)

There are one or two curious points to note in connection with the relaxation of the

---

(97) See Letters Memoranda &c. (K. I. Sangraha), p. 458 ; V. J. Vistára, Vol. V. 179, where also Gopikábái's letter is published ; and compare also Péshvá's Bakhar, pp. 62-4 ; Maráthi Sámrájya Bakhar, p. 93.

(98) See Grant Duff, Vol. II, pp. 120, 168, and compare *inter alia* Bháu Sáhéb's Bakhar, pp. 89 90 ; Péshvá's Bakhar. pp. 61, 64 65. Forrest, pp. 250-1, and 677, shows what was thought of her by the English in those days. But they were prejudiced in favour of Ràghobá Dádá, their ally, and therefore not altogether fair judges of his opponent Gopikábái. But see also Dowson's Elliott, Vol. VIII, pp. 267, 287 ; Forbes's Oriental Memoirs, Vol. I, p. 478.

(99) See Forrest's Selections, Vol. I. p. 725.

rules regarding the taking of food. The first point I take at secondhand from a note by the Editor of the Life of Sháhu (100) written by Malhár Rámráv Chitnis. The Pratinidhi, Parashurám Trimbak, having come under the displeasure of Sháhu on account of his son's having gone over to the Kolhápur interest, was about to be put to death by Sháhu's orders, when Khando Ballál Chitnis hastened to the spot and, interceding for the Pratinidhi, saved his life. (101) From that time forward, it is said that one prominent member of the family of Khando Chitnis was, for a long time, always asked to the *Shrâddha* or anniversary dinners of the Pratinidhi's family, in company with the Bráhmans invited. Two similar departures from strict rule in regard to dinners are mentioned in the Bakhar of the battle of Khardá. After the victory, the Péshvá was taken round by Náná Fadanavis to honour the various Sardárs with a visit. Among others, they called on the two Sardárs of the Sindhiá—Jivbá Dádá and Lakhobá Náná. There the Péshvá was invited to what is called a *farâl,* that is, a

(100) P. 26. I can refer to an original authority, but only from the Prabhu side of the question. See the History of the Chitnis Family in K. P. I. S., p. II, see also K. P. Bakhar, (K. P. I. S.), p. 13 n.

(101) See Bhonslé Bakhar, p. 17; Grant Duff, Vol. I, p. 426.

dinner about which there are fewer ceremonial difficulties than the ordinary preparations. The Péshvá turned to Náná, saying "these people are *Shénvis,* (102) how can their request be granted?" Whereupon Náná said, "the preparations have been made by our Bráhman cooks. What does it matter, if they are *Shénvis*? Jivbá's wishes must not be baulked. He has handled his sword well. Such difficulties with the Sardárs must be overcome." Then the Péshvá and the Bráhmans who accompanied him sat down to the *farál*—the Péshvá taking something only for form's sake, and the rest taking the *farál* in the usual way. From the narrative in the Bakhar, it seems clear that all parties thought that something not in accordance with the prevailing rules was being done, and that the justification or excuse for its being done was found in the political exigencies of the occasion. From Jivbá Dádá's tents, the Péshvá proceeded to those of Parashurám Bháu

(102) P. 20. The Shénvis are called "fish-eating Bráhmans" in Chitraguptá's Life of Shivájí, p. 123, and K. A. Sabhásad's Life, p. 57 (where there are certain paragraphs, pronounced by the Editor on good grounds to be interpolated, which are nevertheless of interest from a historical point of view). The objection of the Péshvá mentioned above was based upon the prevailing custom, which must have originally arisen from the Shénvis being ordinarily a "fish-eating" caste, while other classes of Bráhmans are not such. See also Fryer, p. 190.

Patvardhan. (103) Here, too, the Péshvá had an invitation to stay for dinner. There was, of course, no caste difficulty here, as both parties belonged to the same caste-division. But the Péshvá said to Náná, "Parashurám Bháu is in mourning. (104) What should be done?" Again Náná was up to the occasion and ready with his practical advice. "Bháu's wishes," said Náná, "must not be baulked on such an occasion as this; some way out of the difficulty about the mourning shall be found." (105) Ultimately the Péshvá consented, and he and all his party took their night meal at Parashurám Bháu's camp—Bháu himself sitting apart, and not in the same row with his guests, in consequence of his mourning. The writer of the Bakhar says, that on account of the Péshvá's condescension, Bháu forgot his grief for the loss of his nephew, and told (106) the Péshvá

(103) Khardá Bakhar, p. 20.

(104) Parashurám Bháu's nephew had been killed at the battle of Khardá, and for ten days after his death, his dwelling and all his family would be in a state of ceremonial impurity. See Fryer, p. 101.

(105) This idea is worthy of note.

(106) P. 20 Jivbá Dádá also had expressed himself in terms of similar gratitude. The elder Mádhavráv Péshvá's dining with Janoji Bhonslé, as mentioned in the Lives of the Nâgpur Chitnises (K. P. I. S.), p. 3, does not seem to be a matter of much religious or social significance. It appears from Mr. Forrest's Selections from Bombay State Papers, (Vol. I, p. 162), that the elder Mádhavráv Péshvá once invited Mr. Mostyn "to stay and sup with him," and that Mr.

that the latter's staying to dinner in the house of mourning was an ample reward to him for his labours in the field. (107)

On the next point of this sort to which I now proceed to draw attention, the evidence is not quite as clear as could be wished. Such as it is, however, I will now adduce it. One of the most splendid festivities celebrated during the days of the Péshvá power was on the occasion of the marriage of Savái Mádhavráv. The grand doings are described in much detail in the Péshvá's Bakhar (108). And we have also a Memorandum dated Saké 1704 (A. D. 1782)

Mostyn did so. How the supper went off, and what were the details of the arrangements, one would have liked to know, but no information is forthcoming on that head, as far as I am aware. As to what Westerns think about Indian preparations, see Ovington's Voyage to Surat pp. 295-6, 397; Forbes's Oriental Memoirs, Vol. II, p. 49; Tavernier's Travels, Vol. I, p. 409.

(107) In his recently published Life by Nigudkar, Parashurám Bháu is stated to have been a very pious Hindu. His request to the Péshvá, therefore, is remarkable, as well as Náná's counsel, and the Péshvá's compliance.

(108) See pp. 135-44. The note of the Editor of the Péshvá's Bakhar on this passage seems to me, I confess, hardly to deal fair measure to Mahádji Sindhiá. It is true that Mahádji was in all likelihood not himself really a lover of such exhibitions (See Forrest's Selections, Vol. I, p. XXIX which is presumably based on Malcolm's Central India, Vol. I, p. 125). And doubtless it is, therefore, not unfair to infer that he had an obejct in

containing a most elaborate series of directions as to each one of the innumerable elements making up the "pride, pomp and circumstance" of a glorious

---

arranging for them on this occasion. But the elaborately sinister object attributed to him in the note under reference is scarcely the probable one. There is nothing that I am aware of, in Mahádji's career or character to warrant the imputation, that he wanted to enfeeble the whole of the Deccan Maráthás for his personal aggrandisement. What he probably did aim at was the establishment of an influence on the single individual, Savái Mádhavráv more potent than that of Náná Fadanavis. And he probably sought to secure this by means of striking shows, which would naturally be supposed to be the best passport to such influence with one whom apparently all around him were then treating as still a child. The Péshvá's Bakhar, further, does not indicate that Náná on his part objected in the slightest degree to any of these shows, but rather the contrary. The idea that he must have done so may be correct, but there is no evidence whatever adduced to substantiate it. Such as it is, the evidence seems to me rather to point the other way; so far as the general taste of those days is concerned—though I am not aware of anything sufficiently specific about Náná himself in relation to this point. (See *inter alia* Péshvá's Bakhar, pp. 131, 167, 172, 175, 193; Bháu Sáhéb's Bakhar, pp. 99 130; V. J. Vistára, Vol. V, p. 200; *Ibid*, Vol. X, pp. 6, 7. Chitnis's Sháhu p. 49; Maráthi Sámrájya Bakhar, pp. 87, 102; Péshvá Sakávali, pp. 17, 90; Chitnis's Rájárám, p. 50; Asiatic Researches, Vol. III, p. 24; Ovington's Voyage to Surat, p. 329, *et seq.*; Grant Duff, Vol. II, p. 159; Dowson's Elliott, Vol. VIII, p. 280. For the marriage of Savái Mádhavráv, celebrated without Mahádji having his finger in the pie, Rs. 50,000 were spent on cloth alone, and this was under Náná Fadanavis's management. See Letters, Memoranda &c. (K. I. Sangraha), p. 226. See also in connection with this *Ibid*, pp. 273-74.

marriage, including the perfumery, refreshment, amusements to be provided, the men to superintend them, and so forth. (109) Among other things, the Memorandum directs that Sardárs, Silédárs, Maráthás, Musalmans, Ali Bahádur (110) and others, should be taken after they are assembled together to the house of the bride's father for dinner and for *farál* ; and they should be invited to a *farál* or dinner at the palace on the proper occasions. And again it is said, that the Nabáb, Bhonslé, Holkar, and Silédárs of high position, Sarkárkuns (*sic*) Maráthás and Musalmans, should be invited. And, after determining what is appropriate, they should be taken to the house of the bride's father and to the palace for dinner, and to see the dance. They should be invited, and provisions also should be sent to them. It is not clear from these directions how the various guests—Maráthás, Musalmans, &c.—were accommodated at the time of the dinners and *faráls*, nor how they were served. And, therefore, one cannot be sure that they all sat down together and were served out of the same pots, though this does not seem altogether unlikely.

---

(109) Letters, Memoranda &c. (K. I. Sangraha), pp. 277, 292.

(110) The son of Samshér Bahádur, who was the son of the first Bájiráv by Mastáni.

(111) In any case, however, it seems clear that Musalmans as well as Maráthás sat down to the grand marriage dinners at the palace and at the house of the bride's father; and in this elaborately detailed Memorandum, there is nothing said about their having any separate parts of the houses set apart for them other than those which were used for the Bráhmans invited.

Passing now from this point about dinners, we come to the important point of marriage. And here, too, it appears that the Péshvás on their part initiated a change of custom which, however, failed to get itself established. I am not now referring to Bájiráv's left-handed marriage with Mastáni; but Báláji Bájiráv, who was, of course, of the *Chitpávan* or *Konkanastha* section of the Bráhman caste, married Rádhábái, who belonged to a different section of that caste, viz. *Déshastha*. (112) And it is said, though

(111) See further Letters &c., (K. I. Sangraha), p. 278. In the Péshvá's Bakhar, p. 143, a separate dinner for Musalman guests is mentioned.

(112) Letters, Memoranda &c. (K. I. Sangraha), p. 541, Péshvá Sakávali, p. 18. I have recently had an opportunity, thanks to the kindness of Mr. V. V. Lélé of the Poona Bar, of seeing a modern compilation from miscellaneous sources known as Péndsé's Diary. There, as in the two authorities just adduced, only two marriages of Báláji Bájiráv are mentioned, while reference is also made to Báláji's kept mistresses. There is room, therefore, for reasonable doubt about the statement regarding the Karhádá marriage.

no written authority is forthcoming for the statement, that Báláji had also married a *Karhádá* girl, in order to secure the ultimate complete amalgamation of three of the great sections of the Bráhman community—viz. *Déshasthás*, *Konkanasthás* and *Karhádás*. The object, however, has not been attained, and it is still usual, to put it in the mildest language, to look askance at intermarriages (113) amongst the several subdivisions.

It is curious to notice that even in the days of Péshvá rule, there had come into existence a number of Bráhmans who were unable to help in the performance of ordinary religious ceremonies. In the sketch, already once referred to, of the last days of Parashurám Bháu Patvardhan, we read that after the fuel had been collected for the cremation of the great warrior's corpse, and some *Bhikshuks*, or priestly Bráhmans, had been got together from the village near the place of cremation, the Kárkun, Náro Hari Karandikar, wished to burn the body with the proper *mantrás* and ceremonies, but a good Bráhman could not be secured for the occasion; the *Joshis* of the

(113) They do take place, but on extremely rare occasions. The Jnána Prakásh newspaper says that even dining together was extremely unusual among these three divisions before the times of Bájiráv.

village were sheer dunces; and so the body had to be burnt with an unconsecrated fire (114).

A similar instance of ignorance, perhaps, however, more excusable than this, is recorded in connection with the death of the famous Svámi of Dhávadasi, the *Maháburusha* of Bájiráv I. and others. We read in the Bakhar of Brahméndra Svámi of Dhávadasi, that the attendant Bráhmans performed the ceremonies consequent on his death, with the Ritual Book in their hands. Even with this aid, however, they appear to have blundered, and after they had declared in answer to a question from Sháhu, that the whole of the ceremonial was finished, the Rájá inquired whether their book did not contain any direction about the break-

(114) Letters, memoranda &c., (K. I. Sangraha) p. 300. The statement in Nigudkar's recently published Biography that Parashurám Bháu was burnt with the usual ceremonies (p. 125) is not consistent with the Sketch referred to, which expressly speaks of a *Bhadágni*. The story mentioned by Grant Duff, Vol. III, pp. 185-6 note, about the inhuman treatment of the corpse by the Mahárájá of Kolhápur (which seems to have been merely reproduced by Capt. Robertson, in his Life of Náná Fadanavis, p. 167, without any addition or modification, or apparently corroboration from original documents seen by himself), is not supported by the Sketch of Karandikar. The story offers a curious instance of how error arises from accepting secondhand reports not embodying direct evidence.

ing of the Svámi's skull with a conch-shell—which he had heard was the proper thing to do in the case of a *Sannyási*. The Bráhmans replied that there was a direction to that effect in their book, but that they had overlooked it through inadvertence, and they were thereupon taken up roundly by the Rájá for their ignorance and carelessness. I have said before, that this was, perhaps, a case of more excusable ignorance than was betrayed by the Bráhmans concerned in the death-ceremonies of Parashurám Bháu Patvardhan. These latter ceremonies are every-day ceremonies, which, one would suppose, ought to be familiarly known to all priestly Bráhmans. Those in connection with the death of a *Sannyási*, on the other hand, might well be unfamiliar, as being only of rare occurrence. Still, the ignorance betrayed even on this latter occasion is remarkable, especially when one has regard to the place and the time where the event occurred. It cannot be, that the ignorance was due to there being no demand for that sort of learning in which the men were found deficient. That is a condition of things, of which some sort of indication is, perhaps, beginning to be visible in some parts of the country at the present day. But its existence in the old days to which these events carry us back is not to be assumed. (115) However, whatever may be the true explanation, the facts themselves are worthy of note. (116)

---

(115) I do not think that much weight can be attached, from the point of view from which the above various incidents have been collected to the attack made by one of the Patvardhan chiefs—namely Konherpant—on the *Matha* of the Shankaráchárya Svámi of Sankésvar ; (as to this see V. J. Vistára, Vol. XX, p. 118. ; I presume it is the same incident that is referred to by Forbes at Oriental Memoirs, Vol. II, p. 134, though it is Parashurám Bháu that is named there) ; nor to the plundering raid which seems to have once gone against the priests of Káyagaum [see Letters, Memoranda &c. (K. I. Sangraha) p. 26] ; nor to that which went against Jayarám Svámi's Vadgaum [see Letters &c. (S. K. I. Sangraha). p. 188 ;] nor to the people at large making use of English medicines [see Forrest's Selections p. 550. Forbes's Oriental Memoirs, Vol. III. p. 431, and compare Bhonslé Letters &c. (K. I. Sangraha) p. 79 ; Holkar's Kaifiyat p. 128] ; nor, perhaps, to the fact, mentioned by Tavernier, that some classes of people who would not touch one another under ordinary circumstances, did not scruple to do so in war (see Tavernier Vol. I. pp. 245, 254, and compare Forbes's Oriental Memoirs, Vol. I, p. 231, where he complains of the wretched accommodation he and his party got on one occasion, though under the protection of Rághobá Dádá's escort, in consequence of the Hindus' fear of contamination). Still these facts are not altogether without interest in this connection. I have not seen any original Indian authority about the Sankésvar incident. There is a further reference to it, and explanation of it, at V. J. Vistára, Vol. XXI. p. 285. And see too Malcolm's Central India, Vol. I, pp. 148, 224.

(116) With the above instances of the ignorance of *Bhikshuks*, must be coupled the instances of the laxity of Pandits and Shástris betrayed on the occasion of Shiváji's thread ceremony (as stated in the authorities

In connection with these incidents relating to funeral ceremonies, may be noticed one which is stated to have occurred on the death of the uncle of the famous Bápu Gokhalé viz., Dhondopant Gokhalé. Dhondopant having been killed by a freebooter, named Dhondi Vágh, in an action in which Bápu Gokhalé also was injured and was unable to save his uncle, Bápu cremated the body at the scene of the disaster, and returned to Poona where he wished to perform the residue of the funeral ceremonies enjoined by the customs of the caste. Dhondopant's widow, however, it is said, would not hear of it. She is reported to have spoken very stingingly to Bápu on the occasion, and to have directed that none of the funeral ceremonies should be performed until after Bápu had taken vengeance upon Dhondi Vágh for the slaughter of Dhondopant. The ceremonies were accordingly held in abeyance.

---

referred to in notes 59, 72, 75, supra, and the remarks in the text to which they are attached) and on the occasion of the adoption of Chimnáji Appá by the widow of his nephew Savái Mádhavráv. That adoption was afterwards cancelled; Chimnáji Appá performed penance; and the Shástris who advised the adoption were banished. Robertson's Life of Náná Fadanavis, p. 118, which is based probably on Grant Duff, Vol. III. p. 145. For original authorities see Chitnis's Life of Sháhu, II. p. 67. Letters, Memoranda &c. (K. I. Sangraha) p. 444; see, too, the recent Life of Náná Fadanavis by V. V Kharé, p. 203.

Bápu Gokhalé did soon afterwards get an opportunity of encountering Dhondi Vágh. Dhondi was killed, (117) and his head was carried on a spear's point by Bápu, and shown to Lakshmibái, the widow of Dhondopant Gokhalé. The lady was satisfied, and the countermanded ceremonies were then finished. (118)

There is one incident in the Life of Parashurám Bháu Patvardhan, which is entitled to notice here, although I have not come across any reference to it in any original

(117) Wellington's Letters &c. by Gurwood, p. 9.

(118) Cf. Gáikwád's *Hakikat*, p. 11. The above incident I only know of from Aitihásik Goshti (Historic Anecdotes), one of the many interesting Maráthi works, for which we are indebted to one who has departed from among us since this paper was read, and who was, indeed, a living repertory of interesting and varied information—the late Gopálráv Hari Déshmukh. I have seen no original authority for the story, and it is not mentioned in the recently published Life of Bápu Gokhalé, where it is simply stated that Bápu dertermined, of his own motion, not to put on his turban until after he had wreaked vengeance on Dhondi ; see Life, p. 37. (With this compare Chitraguptá's Shiváji, p. 56, K. A Sabhásad's Ditto p. 35.) There were some comments in the first edition of that Life on Grant Duff's account of the destruction of Dhondi (pp. 98-99) which were *not* conspicuous for *historic* criticism. These are not repeated in the second edition, however, so nothing further need now be said about them. For other instances of woman's stern determination, see Bháu Sáhéb's Bakhar p. 14 ; Malcolm's Central India. Vol I, p. 107; Bernier p. 41 ; Hamilton's East Indies, Vol. I, p. 136 ; also Dowson's Elliott, Vol. VII, p. 2.

document accessible to me. The incident itself is pretty familiar to people in the Maráthá country, but I take the account of it that is given in the biography of Parashurám Bháu recently published by Mr. B. D. Nigudkar. (119) It appears, then, that Parashurám Bháu's eldest daughter, Bayábái, was married into the family of the Joshis of Bárámati. She was only about 7 or 8 years old at the time. And her husband died within about a fortnight after the marriage. She, therefore, became a child-widow according to the usual custom. Some time afterwards, Parashurám Bháu laid the whole of the case of the unlucky girl before the celebrated Rám Shástri, who has been already mentioned in this paper. His heart was touched; and he declared it as his opinion, that there was no objection to the little girl being remarried. Then, Parashurám Bháu sent up the case to Benáres, and the opinion of all the Shástris there was obtained in favour of such remarriage. But after this stage was reached, Parashurám Bháu abandoned his intention of getting the girl remarried, because it was represented to

(119) Pp. 131-2. This book is stated to have been written, after reference to some original unprinted papers; and it is also stated that some of these papers were subsequently examined by Ráv Bahádur M. G. Ranadé, for verifying Mr. Nigudkar's account.

him, that the remarriage of widows was against the custom which had existed for many years, and that it was not advisable for him to run the risk of offending his people by taking a departure from such a custom. The result was that the idea was abandoned. But the incident is, nevertheless, of much historic importance. That such a man as Parashurám Bháu Patvardhan, one of the most prominent men at the Court of the Péshvás, a man who, as his biographer shows, was at heart a full believer in the religion of his ancestors, (120) should seriously contemplate such a departure from established rules, (121) is a thing sufficiently remarkable, when we are considering the nature of the hold which those established rules had upon the conscience of that generation. That so venerable and eminent an authority as Rám Shástri, a man widely respected then and since throughout the Maráthá Empire, should have lent his countenance to that contemplated departure from established usage, makes the incident still

---

(120) *Ibid* pp. 132-4. Comp. Letters &c. (K. I Sangraha) p. 501.

(121) We learn from that most valuable treasure-house of information on the condition of India about 1,000 or 1,200 years ago, viz. Buddhist Records of the Western World, that in the days of Hiuen Thsang widow-marriage was not customary among Hindus (See Vol. I. p. 82).

more remarkable. And it is most remarkable of all, that the Shástris of Benáres should have afforded the support of their unanimous opinion to such a departure. On the other hand, it illustrates the condition of Hindu Society in reference to such a practical departure, that even with the powerful support (122) now indicated, and with the proofs in his hand that the current notions rested on no substantial basis, a man like Parashurám Bháu Patvardhan should, nevertheless, have found himself unable, owing to his surroundings, to take the step to which the kindly impulses of his own heart prompted him.

One other incident of this same class I must here notice, though here again I have not been able to obtain any information about it from any of our own original documents. It relates to a matter about which many members of the Hindu community throughout India may be said to be in some degree exercised at the present day. The only information I have about it is contained in the famous Oriental

---

(122) A writer in the Jnána Prakásh newspaper of Poona asserts that Rám Shátri had died before the Benáres opinion was received; and that the consequent loss of his support prevented Parashurám Bháu from carrying out his original intention.

Memoirs of Forbes (123)—who was in Western India in 1766 and for several years subsequently. Forbes relates, that "two Bráhmans, whom he (*i.e.*, Rághobá Dádá) sent as ambassadors to England, were, on their return to Hindustán, compelled to pass through the sacred *yoni*, or female *lingam*, made of the finest gold. After performing this ordeal, (124) and making valuable presents to the Bráhmans, they were restored to the privileges of their caste, which they had lost, by the

---

(123) See Forbes's Oriental Memoirs, Vol. I, p. 379. From a later part of the same interesting work, we learn, that Rághobá having gone from Surat to Cambay by sea, "many religious Bráhmans and strict professors among the high castes of Hindus, censured Rághobá for undertaking a voyage by sea, in which they alleged he not only deviated from the established laws and customs of his tribe, but thought he acted contrary to the divine injunction." Forbes, Vol. II, p. 8. Those "religious Bráhmans and strict professors," would, therefore, have condemned all their brethren, who for many years past have been voyaging up and down the Indian Coasts, from Ceylon to Karáchi. *Their* condemnation was not confined, as that of their brethren of the present day most illogically and baselessly is practically confined, to a voyage to Europe. Rághobá travelled by sea more than once (See Náráyanráv Péshvá's Bakhar p. 13) ; and Shiváji went by sea to Bédnore. See V. J. Vistára, Vol. IX, p. 132.

(124) A writer in the V. J. Vistára, Vol. XI, p. 235, asserts it to be a well-known fact that Rághobá's emissary Abá Kálé was re-admitted to caste without penance. As usual, no voucher for this well-known fact is adduced. It is not a fact at all according to Forbes's contemporary account.

impurities contracted in travelling through so many polluted countries." It would thus appear, that in those good old days, when the country was to all intents and purposes still under the rule of Bráhman Sovereigns, the sin of crossing the *Kálápáni* was not considered quite inexpiable, and the doctrine now propounded—that a twiceborn person, who goes out on a sea-voyage, cannot be admitted to the "privileges of his caste," *even* after a penance—was not the accepted doctrine of the people, and had not the sanction of the then reigning Péshvá.

As I have brought together so many instances in which the rigours of existing rules appear to have been deliberately relaxed to a greater or less extent, (125) it is right also to point out one or two instances which, in some respects, may be said to present a different appearance to the view. Thus there can be no doubt that the documents before us show many intances of very early marriages in the Péshvá family. (126) Bálájì Bájiráv, for instance, was married when he was 9 years old; Vishvásráv when he was 8; the elder Mádhavráv, 9; Náráyanráv, 10; Savái Mádhav-

(125) Compare also, generally, Chitnis's Life of Rájárám. I, pp. 58, 86; Grant Duff, Vol. I, pp. 322, 373n.

(126) See *inter alia* Péshvá Shakávali, pp. 5, 10 14, 22, 33.

ráv a little over 8. And this was not merely the practice in the Péshvá's family. (127) We find from a brief autobiographical sketch of Náná Fadanavis, that he was married when he was only 10 years old. (128) Again we find a record of more than one remarriage immediately after the death of a first wife. (129) As to widows, there is a curious entry in a chronological list of important events which occurred in the last few years of Péshvá rule. (130) On the 12th of Shrávan Shudda 1729, it is stated that widows were subjected to the shaving opera-

---

(127) See V. J. Vistára, Vol. IX, pp. 41, 51; Chitnis's Rájárám, pp. 44, 52; Rámdás Charitra, pp. 1, 2; Maráthi Sámrájya Bakhar, p. 126, for some other cases. And see, generally, Hamilton's East Indies, Vol. I. p. 158; Ovington's Voyage, pp. 321-4; Fryer, p. 33; Forbes's Oriental Memoirs, Vol. I, p. 73.

(128) Letters, Memoranda &c. (K. I. Sangraha) p. 34. It would seem that this Sketch was not seen by Captain Robertson, Náná's biographer. The original of the Sketch is said to have been taken to England by Mr. Brook; see V. V. Kháré's Life, p. 4. From Mr. Nigudkar's Life of Parashurám Bháu Patvardhan, it appears that Parashurám Bháu was married when he was thirteen years old.

(129) See *inter alia* Péshvá's Bakhar, p. 172; Péshvá Shakávali, pp. 15, 35; Chitnis's Rájárám, II, pp. 3, 57; Sámrájya Bakhar, p. 103; Vinchurkar's Bakhar, p 6.

(130) Letters, Memoranda &c. (K. I. Sangraha) p. 523. See Ovington, pp. 343-4, and Tavernier, Vol. II, p. 209, for some remarks on the custom as prevalent in their days.

tion at the Nágazari in Poona. One would have liked to possess some further information about this hideous performance. Again it appears that a dancing girl's dance was among the entertainments ordinarily provided at marriages; (131) and that not only a man's wives, but even his kept mistresses, (132) sacrificed themselves as *Satis* upon his death.

Looking at the facts and circumstances here collected as a whole, we may say that we get some slight glimpse of the social and religious condition of Maráthá society during the days of the old regime. That many

(131) See *inter alia* Maráthi Sámrájya Bakhar pp.) 49, 102-4; Péshvá's Bakhar, pp. 139, 161; V. J. Vistára, Vol. XIII, pp. 203-238. See also the Life of Rávji Apâji (K. P. I. S.) pp. 27, 63, and compare Forbes's Oriental Memoirs Vol. I. p. 81. This has precedents of quite respectable antiquity. See Kálidásá's Raghuvansa, Canto III, Stanza 19. Tavernier often mentions such entertainments; see *inter alia* Vol. I, pp. 71, 87, 158, 259, 289, and compare Scott's Deccan, Vol. I, pp. 29, 77; Forbes (Oriental Memoirs, Vol. II, p. 53) mentions that loose women used to be in the Maráthá Camps, though Shiváji's rule was absolute against it. See Chitraguptá's Life, p. 36 (also p. 150), Fryer's Travels, p. 176; see too, however, Chitragupta p. 162.

(132) See the Bhonslè Bakhar pp. 79, 119; Péshvá Shakávali, p. 10, compare Dowson's Elliott, Vol. I, p. 6; and Bernier, p. 310. Self-immolation by widows was controlled by the Musalman rulers of India. See Ovington, p. 343; Tavernier, Vol. I, p. 210; and see Lord William Bentinck (Rulers of India Series), p. 104. From the Bhonslé Letters &c. (K. I. Sangraha) p. 12, it appears that on one occasion the thirteen wives of a man all sacrificed themselves together as *Satis*.

things which exist now also existed then, of course, goes without saying. (133) That the Bráhmanical system existed then in greater strength than at present, is also what might naturally have been anticipated. But that there should have been so many actual departures from traditionary rule, that there should have been such schemes contemplated as some of those which have been here noticed, are facts which are not in harmony with the notion that prevails in some quarters, that laxity in these matters began with the introduction under British rule of Western ideas into this country. (134) To my

---

(133) In Mr. Forrest's Selections from Bombay State Papers, one can see many instances of business being delayed by reason of weddings, and formal mournings, Holi celebrations, and unlucky constellations. See *inter alia* pp. 129, 130, 145, 146, 149, 150, 159, 175, 596. See also Forbes's Oriental Memoirs, Vol. II, p. 22; Dowson's Elliott, Vol. VII, p. 296. : At Prof. Forrest's Bombay Selections, Vol. I, p. 489, we find one example of the constellations being given to go-by when met by firmness on the part of the British Officer with whom business had to be transacted. See also Forbes's Oriental Memoirs, Vol. III, p. 473, for another similar case. At Bháu Sáhéb's Kaifiyat, p. II, we have a recorded instance of how an enterprise commenced under favourable conditions of the constellations, nevertheless resulted in failure.

(134) In the Káyastha Prabhunchi Bakhar, p. 10, it is stated that the ordinary conduct of all castes was spiritually unclean under Mahomedan rule. Bráhmans did not observe the rules about what to eat and what not. See also the opinions of the Benáres Pandits, at pp. 17-8. See further Káyastha Prabhunchyá Itihásáchin Sádhanén

mind, the various items above set out indicate a relaxation which had commenced long before that period. And when we have regard to the causes of the relaxation, as indicated in one or two of these instances, the conclusion which they suggest is, that the surrounding conditions, even in the days of the Maráthá power, were too strong for the dominion of rules which had had their birth under quite other and different conditions. Originally, I suppose, the incompatibility manifested itself only in certain special instances. But once the solvent, so to say, is applied in that way at one point, similar results sometimes follow even at other points, though the conditions are not equally directly favourable.

It will have been noticed that some of the instances above given, of departure from the old rules of conduct, are instances of deliberate departure, consciously made in view of the existing conditions, while others cannot be so clearly traced to a conscious initiative, but seem to form part of what I have called a general relaxation of the

---

(Grámanya) P. 13; V. J. Vistára, Vol. IX, pp. 31-3: Chitraguptá's Shiváji pp. 97, 137; Sri Siva Kávya, Part I, pp. 51-2, 107, and compare N. Macleod's Peeps at the Far East p. 266, for some remarks by an outsider on this topic.

rigours of traditionary bonds. In both respects, I am disposed to think, further progress, up to a certain point, would have been achieved, and achieved with comparative ease, if the sceptre of Maháráshtra had not passed away from the hands of the Péshvás.. Under indigenous rulers, whose fundamental rules of Government have been illustrated above, such progress would have come directly, and perhaps also indirectly, with less friction, (135) than under a foreign power like the British, governed by the principles which it has laid down for itself; although, no doubt, the silent force of education in Western science and art, in Western history and literature, which the British have brought to bear, must necessarily have been entirely absent under indigenous rule (136.)

The late Sir Henry Sumner Maine pointed many years ago, that the operations of British Courts of Justice had resulted in the arrest of the further development of Hindu Law. (137) It may with truth be said, that the passive influence of British admi-

(135) Compare the remarks, of somewhat similar purport, in Sir H. S. Maine's Village Communities (3rd Ed.) pp. 46-7.

(136) This would have been absent in both its aspects as indicated by Sir H. S. Maine in his Village Communities, p. 273, and also pp. 270 and 288.

(137) See Village Communities pp. 45-7.

nistration generally, has had a somewhat similar effect on the general social development of the Hindus. It is not easy as yet to analyse fully the causes which have so far led or are leading to such a result; nor would this be a proper place to institute such an analysis. But speaking broadly, it would appear, that the general effect of British administration has been to render feeble the various forces, which were, in old days, working from within the community itself as a community; (138) while, on the other hand, individualism has become, or is becoming, more and more the prevailing force. Náná Fadanavis, for instance, when the occasion arose, gave advice as to what was required to be done, even in defiance of what was supposed to be right according to existing traditions. And the Péshvá acted on such advice, the Bráhmans about him followed the example, and nobody apparent-

---

(138) In the Káyastha Prabhunchi Bakhar (K. P. I. S.) p. 9, we read that a dispute having occurred in these parts between the Bráhmans and the Káyastha Prabhus, the matter was referred to the Pandits of Benáres, and on their decision in favour of the Káyasthas, *all* people in Western India commenced to act in accordance with that decision, notwithstanding all the previous dissensions. Some recent doings, however, of a different aspect also find their parallel in events of the days of Savái Mádhavráv. See Káyastha Prabhunchyá Itihásáchin Sádhanén (Grámanya) p. 7.

ly raised any storm about it. It does not appear, that the way out of the difficulty which Náná said *would be found* after the act itself was done, (139) had even to be sought after. If it had been necessary to seek after it, it would doubtless have been found—the community being still endowed with vitality as a community; and it would, no doubt, have been a way of the same nature as is indicated by the various instances we have stated. The old rules would, by common, even if tacit, consent, have been gradually relaxed, and in process of time custom would have sanctified everything. Such a process, I believe, is what might have been witnessed under Péshvá, and even under what may be called, in the narrower sense, Maráthá rule. But such a process hardly takes place at our present stage of progress, or at all events is incomparably more slow and tedious in

(139) See notes (103) and (104) *Supra.* Yet Náná himself, it must never be forgotten, was not a sceptic nor free-thinker. See Letters, Memoranda &c. (K. I. Sangraha), pp. 34, 39, and V. V. Kharé's Life, p. 166, (where the Poet Moropant is quoted in proof of his piety ; see also Sri Siva Káyva, XVI, 27.) He was in truth, a thoroughly pious Hindu. The pious of the present day, on the other hand, are still digging into the depths of the Smritis &c. to disinter texts justifying a voyage to England, or saying with decrepit helplessness—the thing is forbidden, and there is an end of the matter as far as we are concerned.

its operation, wherever British influence is in other respects powerful. The late Mr. Krishna Shástri Chiplonkar, thirty years ago, having been supposed to have eaten fruit at the table of a European friend (140) was hauled over the coals in a community where he was a leader of thought. A similar thing has occurred since with similar results. It has been said that the first event retarded progress, and whether that is true or not, and whether there has been progress since then or not, it is perfectly clear, that such progress as there has been is extremely slow. And on the other hand it has certainly disclosed the existence of persons, to whom the real gist of the movement under Péshvá rule is either unknown or unacceptable.

I must not, however, permit myself to continue these reflections any further. The main purpose of this paper is to piece together some features of the past, from the scanty and desultory materials available. This having been done, the lessons to be drawn from a study of those features must be allowed to remain over for consideration and discussion elsewhere. I will only, in conclusion, add one line of explanation. The incidents here

---

(140) See the incident referred to in Dr. Norman Macleod's Peeps at the Far East, p. 68n and p. 375.

collected have been drawn from the available records, without any attempt to discriminate between those records which are contemporaneous and those which are not such. It must, of course, be admitted, that many, even most, of these records are not really contemporaneous. But in dealing with such a theme as that to which this paper is devoted, it has not been thought necessary to take any account of that circumstance. In any case, these records are of value on the principle which Grote applied to the older Greek writings—"the curtain *is* the picture." And as most if not all the documents drawn upon belong apparently to the period of the ancient régime, their special evidentiary value, as regards the special incidents for which they are relied on, has not appeared to me to be a subject necessary to be dealt with as part of the present inquiry.

---

* This paper was read before the Deccan College Union on the 17th September 1892 by the late Mr. Justice K. T. Telang.